Make some noise for the Bluebirds!
An illustrated, fans eye view of Cardiff City FC & Ninian Park.

gary wharton

lushington PUBLISHING

for gary and shaun

Published in 2005 by lushington publishing, cardiff.

typography + page design: **gary wharton**> garywha@yahoo.com

Printed + bound by Cromwell Press Ltd, Aintree Avenue,
White Horse Business Park, Trowbridge, Wiltshire BA14 0XB.
Website www.cromwellpress.co.uk

ontents

In 1899 Riverside F.C was founded

and a few years later was amalgamated with Riverside Albion. As the latter, a practice match was arranged at Sophia Gardens to gage local interest in a football side. With Bartley Wilson in a pivotal role, he had set about the creation of a football team from the shell of Riverside cricket club. Bart and a group of fellow sports enthusiasts sought to form the town's first professional football, or 'soccer' team, as it was nicknamed at the time.

By 1900 the club were playing in the Cardiff and District League in a kit consisting of chocolate and amber quarters and black shorts. Advancing to 1908 and Cardiff City Football Club becomes a reality; but the necessity for a ground becomes paramount as interest in the project blooms. Competitive matches against the likes of Crystal Palace, Bristol City and Middlesborough cements the introduction of Cardiff into the second division of the Southern League in 1910. The City corporation allocated waste land on Sloper road which required substantial work before it would be suitable and safe for public attendance.

In 1905 Cardiff was officially recognized as a city and the club was nearing legitimised status. In 1908 Cardiff City AFC was acknowledged as the new name for the Riverside club. However, the club still maintained its amateur status. It was in April 1910 that a limited company was formed and Cardiff City Football Club turns professional. The club plays two friendlies / exhibition games to test public reaction, the Arms Park and a local rugby ground on Newport road being venues chosen. Aston Villa, the Champions of the English League of 1909/ 10 play the first match at Ninian Park on Thursday 1 September 1910. Cardiff lose 1-2 but the fixture marked the start of something special which continues to enthral thousands come rain or shine, promotion or relegation. Hopefully this book shines a light on just why this is the case.

Aston Villa

Bristol City

Crystal Palace

Middlesborough

season 1910/11

Cardiff in Southern League Division Two; finishing the season a credible 4th.

The club became a limited company in April 1910 with a share issue of 10 shillings [50p]. The season marked City's introduction in to the Welsh Cup competition. Cardiff changed their colours from a lovely chocolate and amber to a more sobering blue for this season. They also put out a team for the Glamorgan League, from which they withdraw at the end of the season. Managed by player/boss Davy McDougall, the ground has a new wooden grandstand built. The friendly v Aston Villa in September 1910 is to be the first of a dozen such matches at the ground.

Cup competitions: Defeats at Merthyr Town and Ton Pentre in the FA and Welsh Cup.

Best result: 7-1 v Chesham at Ninian Park.

Attendances:12,000 v Merthyr Town [City lose 0-1]. A Wales v Scotland international sees 20,000 at Ninian Park.

season 1911/12

Cardiff finish third in the league.

Cup competitions: eliminated by Merthyr Town again in the FA Cup. Better result in the Welsh Cup which Cardiff win 3-0 in a replay v Pontypridd. Fred Stewart, recently manager at Stockport County, is appointed full-time secretary-manager at Ninian Park.

Best result: 5-1 defeat of Cwn Albion.

However, a 6-0 is inflicted away at Plymouth Argyle in one of a number of friendly fixtures arranged this season.

Attendances: 15,000 see City beaten 1-2 by Merthyr Town. Merthyr were originally formed in 1908 and elected to the Southern League Division Two in 1909.

season 1912 / 13

City win promotion to the Southern League Division One.
They dominate there, starting with a 1-1 draw with debutants Swansea Town at their newly constructed Vetch Field ground. Newport County are formed as a professional club and upon visiting Ninian Park are defeated 2-0. City remain unbeaten all season up until the Swansea match in the Welsh Cup semis.
Cup competitions: k.o'd by the Blues of Southend United in the FA Cup and 4-2 by Swansea at home in the Welsh Cup.
Best result: 9-0 v Ebbw Vale, watched by 7,000 at Ninian Park.
Attendances 21,000 see City beat Luton Town in a home match.

season 1913 / 14

A hard one for the City finishing tenth in the top division.
Cup competitions: flattened by Swansea Town in the FA Cup and defeated by Oswestry in the 3rd round of the Welsh Cup.
Best result: Three 3-0 victories at Ninian Park. The Eagles of Crystal Palace mash City 4-0 in January 1914.
Attendances: 20,000 v Plymouth Argyle, winning 2-1 at home.
City played in the South West Combination League, added 21 friendlies and more up until the cessation of the first world war.

Above: Crystal Palace, Southend United and Luton Town insignia.

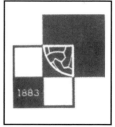

Above: Bristol City and Bristol Rovers insignia.

1914/15 + war years

Again a struggle for the club. Finishing 3rd but the Great War starts and all football is suspended. Bristol City beat the Bluebirds in the FA Cup 2-0.

Best Result: 7-0 destruction of Bristol Rovers watched by 10,000 at Ninian Park. Watford beat Cardiff 3-2 on New years day 1915.

Attendances: 16,000 see the 3-0 defeat of Swindon Town in October.

season 1919/20

Cardiff finish 4th in Division One. Cardiff City FC join the Football League in February 1920. Back then, the Bluebirds had a well-held reputation in the game for their good sportsmanship. They became the first Welsh club to join the league upon being elected to join the redrawn Second Division in May. City had previously played in the Southern League. Fred Keenor nabs their first goal in the opening fixture in the new league being with Stockport. Merthyr Tydfil, Newport County and Swansea Town are all elected to the Third Division in this season.

Cup competitions: Welsh Cup winners 2-1 v Wrexham after defeating Swansea Town in the semis. Put out of the FA Cup by Bristol City in front of 32,432.

Best result: a 6-1 demolition of Northampton Town occurs at Ninian Park.

Attendances: 25,000 see City lose 0-2 v Plymouth and 37,000 away at Wolves whilst 24,371 sets a new attendance record for the Swansea game which Cardiff won 1-0.

season 1920/21

Cardiff finish 2nd in Division Two. A marvellous campaign for the Bluebirds with promotion to Division One achieved. The club had been successful in being elected to the Football League in May 1920 and there was no stopping their progress. The team lose only 8 times and win 24 out of 42 matches; completing the 'double' over Wolves and Leeds.

Fred Stewart, the then-present Cardiff manager, faced his old side Stockport where his Bluebirds side inflict a 5-2 defeat.

City defender and Irish international, Ernest 'Bert' Smith scored the first goal for the club in the division, a 2-1 away defeat at Aston Villa.

Cup competitions: City reached the semi-finals of the FA Cup only to lose in a replay staged at Old Trafford v Wolves by 1-3.

Future skipper, Fred Keenor, scores from the penalty spot.

Best result: A 5-2 v Stockport plus 3-1 beatings away to Pontypridd and Bury.

Attendances: huge figures for many matches. The largest being 45,000 for City's 1-0 Cup victory v Chelsea.

season 1921/22

City finish 4th in Division One in their first season in the top flight. Six Welsh clubs playing in the Football League: Cardiff City, Swansea Town, Newport County, Wrexham, Merthyr Tydfil and Aberdare Athletic. The new Canton stand opens with an admission price of 3 shillings. Bluebirds defence heralded / lauded for its excellence, with 19 wins in 42 games played. However, at the season's start, Cardiff would lose all 6 of their first games and let 13 goals in against 3 scored. A half dozen Cardiff players are selected for international duties this season, namely Keenor/Davies/Evans for Wales, Farquharson and Smith for Ireland and Blair for Scotland. Cup competitions: Beaten by Spurs in an FA Cup 4th round replay following a 1-1 draw at Ninian Park watched by 51,000.

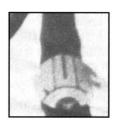

The Welsh Cup belongs to Cardiff following a 2-0 defeat of Ton Pentre. The Bluebirds also win the South Wales & Monmouthshire FA Cup. Best result: Put six past Bradford City at Ninian Park with the Splott-born, City man Len Davis collecting the first City hat-trick. Arsenal are beaten by 4-3, also at home. Aston Villa beat the Bluebirds both home and away whilst Newcastle United are scalped at Ninian Park. Attendances: 56,000 see City's first match in the top league played at Ninian Park. The Bluebirds lose 1-0 to Tottenham Hotspur. City gain their first win at home, after four attempts, v Middlesborough.

City finish 9th in Division One. Cup competitions: Beaten again by Tottenham Hotspur in the FA Cup. Win the Welsh Cup 3-2 v Aberdare. Best result: 6-1 home obliteration of Chelsea highlighted by a Len Davis hat trick; the first of two that season. Jimmy Gill and Joe Clenell also hit the net many times for City. Villa and Arsenal are also seen off at the Bluebirds' ground.With league fixtures providing a tendency of teams meeting each other home and away in consecutive games, Chelsea v City produces a 1-1 draw followed a week later by a healthy 6-1 rout at Ninian Park.

Attendances: 50,000 see Spurs come to Ninian Park and take away a 2-3 win. Cardiff and Spurs play each other seven times in the course of two years with City not winning!

City runners-up in Division One. Managed still by Fred Stewart, Cardiff miss out on the title to Huddersfield Town on goal aggregate alone after both teams had finished on 57 points. A missed penalty away at Birmingham on the last Saturday of the season by Len Davis meant the sides would draw 0-0. Incredibly, and such a decision has never been repeated, Cardiff lost out on the title by .024 goal average!
A run of 11 unbeaten games at the beginning of the season exemplifies the winning ways of City during the campaign.
Bert Smith leaves the club at the end of the season and joins another old Cardiff boy, Fred Pagnam, at Watford.
Cup competitions: 50,000 are at Man City's Maine Road ground to watch City beaten by a single goal in the 4th round of the FA Cup. Newport County finally overcome the Bluebirds in the Welsh Cup after two replays.
Best result: A 4-0 win at Ninian Park takes care of the mighty Gunners [Arsenal], marked by a Gill hat trick. City man Len Davis nets on four

occasions away at West Bromwich Albion. Attendances: 54,000 see the visit of Spurs.

season 1924/25

The Bluebirds finish 11th in Division One. Cup competitions: A 1-0 FA Cup Final defeat at the hands of Sheffield United. City beaten by a single goal v Swansea in the Welsh Cup.
Best result: 4-0 v Burnley at Ninian Park.
Attendances: just over 50,000 attend the 2-1 FA Cup win v Leicester City in Cardiff.

season 1925/26

City finish a mediocre 16th in Division One. Fred Stewart managed the Bluebirds in a dull season campaign. However, the club had some 16 internationals players.

Cup competitions: Merthyr Town and Newcastle United take care of any Cardiff City optimism in the Welsh Cup & FA Cup that season.
Best result: 5-2 win v Leicester City at Ninian Park in November. Eleven goals are put past Cardiff away at Sheffield United. United had beaten the Bluebirds in the FA Cup Final of 1925. City also bashed 0-5 and 3-6 against Arsenal and Blackburn respectively. Jimmy Nelson makes history as the first Cardiff player sent-off in a match v Newcastle United.
Attendances: Despite the depression across the country 42,000 see the eventful Newcastle game in the opening match of the season.

season 1926/27

Cardiff run-in the season in 14th place. The Bluebirds win the FA Cup, Charity Shield and the Welsh Cup this season. With the FA Cup Final taking place on the April 23rd, City had to play eight times in that month alone; 3 games in the space of five days leading up to the Wembley match.

opposite:
Sheffield United, Burnley, Leicester, Blackburn and Arsenal.

Tramways ran directly to Ninian Park for the first time and made journey to the ground easy and convenient for supporters. The FA Cup Final is the first BBC sound commentary to be broadcast live over the wireless. Hughie Ferguson, a Scotsman at Ninian Park creates a goal scoring record that was to last for many, many decades with a total of 32 league and cup goals put away this season alone.

Cup competitions: 1-0 win in the FA Cup Final v Arsenal on St George's Day! 2-0 Welsh Cup winners v Rhyl. The referee that day, W.F Bunnell wore a bow tie and the Arsenal 'keeper, Dan Lewis was a Welsh international. 250,000 greet the victorious Bluebirds return home. Best result: a 6-1 drubbing of Ebbw Vale in Welsh Cup. Derby County smash City 6-3 and Newcastle hit 5 at St James's Park.

Attendances: 49,000+ for an FA Cup match against Bolton Wanderers. Whilst another match v Chelsea, this time a 0-0 FA Cup tie, is attended by 70,184 at Stamford Bridge. The replay at Ninian Park sees City and win 3-2 watched by 47,850.

season
1927/28

The Bluebirds finish 6th in league. With the previous season producing an astronomical fruition of success, the start of the new season proved a letdown; 7 games played and not a win. Cup competitions: Beaten in FA Cup 5th round 2-1 by Nottingham Forest. City winners of the Welsh Cup, 2-0 v Bangor. The Bluebirds beat Corinthians in the FA Charity Shield at Stamford Bridge in October. Best result: 7-0 v Burnley at home in September. With a 4-0 victory v Huddersfield Town at Ninian Park making amends for an 8-2 whacking in the away game to the eventual champions. Derby put 7 past the Bluebirds at the Baseball ground.

Attendances: 35,000 watch the City beat Newcastle United 3-1 at home.

season
1928/29

The Bluebirds are relegated to Division Two. A hefty 21 out of 42 games are lost whilst a mere eight matches are won all season. The Grangetown stand opens.

Cup competitions: Cardiff defeated in the Welsh Cup Final 3-0 v Connah's Quay Nomads. Aston Villa destroy the City 6-1 in the 3rd round of the FA Cup.

Best result: Hughie Ferguson scores five goals in the 7-0 home walkover of Burnley.

Attendances: 51,242 watch the City beaten by Villa in the cup. The Bluebirds are relegated to Division Two. A hefty 21 out of 42 games are lost with only eight matches won all season.

season 1929/30

City finish 8th in Division Two. 'Happy days are here again' echoes to the arrival of the City players played by a brass band sited near the players tunnel. (The irony being that during the 1930s City were at their lowest ebb!) The brass band was introduced at the ground on match days, from this season onwards with the crowd urged to join in. A fire occurs in the stand at Ninian Park causing much damage.

Cup competitions: ko'd by Sunderland in the FA Cup and Welsh Cup final draw replay held over until next season.

Best result: 5-1 v Bury in the final game of the season see by 8000 of the Ninian Park faithful. A 6-2 away friendly in April v Swansea Town leaves a bitter taste. The Swans beat City at their ground 1-0 also.

Attendances: 30,000 at City see local derby v Swansea in an early 0-0 draw. Massive away attendances at Liverpool and Sunderland. City score a total of 43 goals in 42 games. The defence concede 59, the lowest in the Division.

season 1930/31

City relegated to Division Three South. Cardiff lose 25 games and win only 8 all season. Fred Keenor makes his final appearance in a City shirt. City are bottom of the division with three games remaining, Swansea near also but manage a win in their last game of the season thus avoiding relegation. Another Welsh club, Newport County will fail in their re-election to the Football League also.

Cup competitions: Rhyl beaten 4-2 in replayed Welsh Cup final. Early exit in the other tournament by Brentford.

Best result: 7-3 annihilation in the Welsh Cup of Barry Town. Conversely, City battered 7-0 away to Preston.

Attendances: 41,000 watch the 2-2 away draw with Spurs in April.

Left: Bury, Sunderland and Preston NE insignia.

season 1931/32

City finish 9th in Division Three South. Cup competitions: Bradford see off the Bluebirds by 2-0 scoreline in an FA Cup tie between the sides. Best result: 8-0 against Enfield in the FA Cup and a massive 9-2 walloping of Thames Association at Ninian Park in February. Former City scorer Len Davies makes the score sheet for the visitors.
Attendances: 18,343 for a cup match with the Bantams of Bradford. Lowest finds 2000 souls for a Q.P.R 0-4 defeat in November. Six out of 42 League games peak at 10,000+.

October for the first league meeting between the sides. Cardiff lost 3-1 in front of a crowd of 12,000.
Cup competitions: defeats in the first round and semi-finals of the FA Cup and Welsh Cup respectively.
Best result: 6-0 Ninian Park beating of Northampton Town.
Attendances: 14,000 away at Luton see an 8-1 drubbing.

season 1932/33

Cardiff finish 19th in Division Three South. Fred Stewart in charge for his final season at Ninian Park. His Bluebirds lose nearly double the amount of games won. Billy Hardy, with the club since 1920 leaves to take up a management role with Bradford. Hardy played more than 400 matches as a Bluebird. City meet Newport County at Ninian Park in

season 1933/34

City finish bottom of Division Three. In a space of three years the club slip from the first to third division and as a consequence, have to apply to football league for re-admission.
The 63-year-old Bart-Wilson becomes temporary manager of the Bluebirds following the resignation of Fred Stewart. He is replaced by Ben Watts-Jones. Out of a total of 42 games City win 9 and lose 27 with a meagre 24 points collected. Two 6-2 defeats away at Gillingham and Swindon Town.

Cup competitions: out in initial round of the FA Cup and lose to Bristol City in the Welsh Cup.
Best result: a 4-0 home victory clips the wings of Crystal Palace.
Attendances: 16,175 v Newport County see a 1-1 in October.

season 1934/ 35

Bluebirds finish 19th in Division Three. City narrowly avoid relegation by three places: Gillingham, Southend United and Newport County do not. Reg Pugh is recorded as one of the youngest Welsh players ever selected for the City first team. Born in Aberaman in 1917 he made his home debut v Newport County in October 1934 and played for the club up until 1938 and then seems to have left the football scene. City favourite tom Farquharson leaves the club at the end of the season.
Cup competitions: out in FA Cup first round and 7th round of the Welsh Cup.
Best result: 5-0 drubbing of Exeter City with Reg Keating getting his name on the score sheet 4 times! Crystal Palace squash City 6-1.
Attendances: 20,000 see the opening match of the season at Ninian Park, a 2-1 win over Charlton Athletic on 28 August.

season 1935/ 36

City finish a dire 20th in the Third Division.
Cup competitions: No luck in either the Welsh or FA Cup competitions for the Bluebirds managed by Ben Watts-Jones.
Best result: Exeter City defeated 5-2 at Ninian Park. Two 5-1 away defeats recorded at Coventry City and Queens Park Rangers.
Attendances: 20,000 see the third match of the season, the second at Ninian Park.

season 1936/ 37

The Bluebirds reside at 18th in the league. A fire in the main stand at Ninian Park results in the original 1910 grandstand being destroyed. A botched burglary following the Cup defeat by Grimsby Town in January was blamed. Apparently, the thieves were after the gate receipts for the match, watched as it was by over 36,000. On April Fools Day, Watts-Jones quits and takes up a position on the CCFC board. Bill Jennings, coach and former Bolton Wanderers / Wales

international, takes over in April 1937.
Cup competitions: beaten by Barry Town in the Welsh Cup and Grimsby in the FA Cup.
Best result: a 4-1 win v Aldershot in April.
Heavy defeats from Luton Town [1-8], Southend [1-8], Brighton [2-7] and Q.P.R beat them 0-6.
Attendances: good despite the on-field results.

season 1937/38

City 10th in Division Three South.
Ben Watts-Jones resigns as Cardiff City manager and retakes a role on the club board. Bill Jennings is brought in as a replacement.
Cup competitions: flop in both the Welsh and FA Cups.
Best result: 5-2 v Torquay. Debutant Jimmy Collins makes his mark by collecting a hat-trick. Collins is signed from Liverpool by new boss Jennings.
Attendances: 42,000 see City play Newcastle in the FA Cup, eventually losing the replay 1-4. A Wales v England international at Ninian Park in October attracts 55,724.

Danny Malloy:
Central defender with City and always in amongst the goalmouth action which consequently resulted in his record of putting in 14 own-goals as a player!

Team badges, top left to right:
Grimsby Town, Gillingham, Charlton Athletic, Coventry City, Aldershot and Brighton.

season 1938/ 39

The Bluebirds finish 13th in the league. The latest Cardiff City chairman brings in Cyril Spiers to manage the club in April '39 with Bill Jennings finishing. All leagues were suspended with the on-set of the Second World War in September 1939. Newport County, then managed by Billy McCandless beat Cardiff 3-0 at Ninian Park and 2-1 at Somerton Park in the league.

Cup competitions: beat Newport Co in the Welsh Cup but lose 2-1 in the final to South Liverpool. Newcastle United win 4-1 in a 4th round replay tie in the FA Cup.

Best result: 5-0 whitewash of Bournemouth at Ninian Park. Conversely, Walsall beat City 6-3 at their place.

Attendances: 55,724 attend the Wales v England fixture in October '38 with Wales 4-2 victors. 30,000 kick-off the season at home to Exeter. 39,113 see a 1-2 win by Newport County, a team that had already scalped City.

the war years

A period that is not to be seriously considered in terms of results and status due to a proliferation of 'guest' players. These were incorporated at most clubs due to playing staff being called up for service.

City finish 5th in the South West League in 1940. Six goals put past Swindon Town in the League Cup.

1941/ 42

City finish 3rd in the South West League. Eight put past Swindon Town in the War Cup.

1942/ 43

City finished third in the West League. Attendances during the season are no more than 3,000.

However, 5,000 watch City against Swansea Town in a 2-2 draw at Ninian Park. The match is a game from the North Cup competition.

1943/44

City finish second in the West League. Defeated in the West Cup Final 4-2 on aggregate to Bath City.

1944/45 - Cardiff win the West League. 35,000 spectators at Ninian to see the mighty Wolves defeated 2-1 by the Bluebirds in a cup tie.

Opposite:
Torquay, Walsall and Bournemouth badges.

**Wales 2 v Israel 0 -
international match
at Ninian Park**
Israeli keeper Chodoroff was
involved in a heavy challenge
with John Charles resulting in
concussion, broken nose and a
sprained shoulder for the former.
Charles brushed himself off and
ran back up the pitch unaware
of the severity of his opponent's
injuries. The match was a World
Cup qualifier 2nd leg played at
Ninian Park and including City
boys Harrington and Hewitt in
the Welsh side.

seasons 1945/ 46

'Man-to-man passing,
with always 1 player,
and often 2, in an
unmarked position to
receive the ball.
Tip-top attack, but a doubtful defence.'
Sportswriter Ivan Sharpe describing the post-
war Dinamo Moscow. City runners-up in
Division Three South. With the war over, the
football started again and consisted of a
League North, League South, League Three
North, League Three South. Cardiff played in
Division Three South whilst both Newport
County and Swansea Town are in League South.
'Showing wonderful pluck, Bill Rees, the Cardiff
City footballer, played throughout the second
half...with seven stitches in his head...'
Sports report in the SW Echo, 6 October, 1945.
Injured following his scoring of a goal via a
diving header, Rees refused to be left out of
the game and played the second half which
City lost 3-2 at Bristol City! The 1945/ 1946
season was the first post-war campaign and
saw the visit of the mighty Dinamo Moscow in
a November friendly. City lost 1-10 in a greatly
entertaining match.
Cup competitions: Watford bashed 7-1 in
qualifying round of the Third Division South
Cup tournament.
Best result: Bournemouth 9-3 at Ninian Park
with Rees getting four. Stan Richards collects a

hat trick v Bristol Rovers in a Cup match.
Attendances: 28,000 are unfortunate enough to witness Bristol City inflict a 4-2 defeat at Ninian Park

season 1946/47

'It was lovely when we won the title.' Fred Stansfield, City captain that lead the side to the Third Division championship. Many local players in the City first team that collected the title that season. Former City boss Cyril Spiers, now at Norwich, finds himself facing the Bluebirds in the first game of the season at Carrow road. His Canaries beat City 2-1 but back at Ninian Park they are trounced 6-1 by McCandless' Bluebirds. The City team consisted mainly of 10 Welsh players doing the business. Stan Richards, City's main goal-scorer nets 30 in 34 appearances. In June '47 Cardiff were given the Third Division championship following a 1-0 win against Leyton Orient. They finished 9 points clear of the 'super hoops' of Queens Park Rangers after winning 30 out of the 42 games. Severn rivals Bristol City finish in 3rd position behind Q.P.R and Cardiff.
Cup competitions: nothing.
Best result: the 6-1 mashing of Norwich City in which Stan Richards scores a hat-trick. Bryn Allen does the same in a 6-2 home defeat of Northampton Town in January.

Opposite: Northampton, Norwich and Sheff Weds.

Attendances: a new Third Division attendance record is set as 51,621 are present for the City v Bristol City 1-1 draw in April. 48,000 watch a 2-2 v eventual league runners-up, Q.P.R.

season 1947/ 48

City finish a decent 5th in Division Two. Ticket prices increase to three shillings for the Canton stand and two for the terraces. Whilst on the pitch, the Bluebirds strip changes from all blue to a blue with white sleeves. Cyril Spears returns from sojourn as Norwich City boss. Some new ground improvements are completed at Ninian Park this season also, including a player's tunnel. Cardiff-born Ron Stitfall makes his full debut v Chesterfiled.
Cup competitions: 48,000 see Sheffield Wednesday knock Cardiff out of the 3rd round of the FA Cup by 2-1.
Attendances: for the visit of Newcastle United, 50,000 watch a 1-1. £9,000 spent on Ninian Park improvements including a player's tunnel, rebuilding and extending of the grandstand.

Cardiff finish 4th in Division Two, having collected 4 points more than last season.

Cup competitions: k.o'd FA Cup by Derby County. Welsh Cup semi-final defeat by Merthyr Tydfil seen by 22,000.

Best result: 6-1 battering of Brentford at Ninian Park in December.

Attendances: A decent season for the club was highlighted by just over 56,000 against Spurs. City beaten 1-0. 70,718.Incredibly, 70,718 squeeze in to Aston Villa's ground to watch City lose 2-1 in February.

City finish 10th in Division Two.

Cup competitions: City beaten by Swansea and Leeds in the Welsh and FA Cup.

Attendances: 53,099 see City flop in 5th round of FA Cup. Bluebirds squash Swansea 1-0 watched by 57,510 at Ninian Park in August. However, Swansea flatten City 5-1 at theirs in a return league fixture. Nearly 60,000 see City beaten 2-0 at White Hart Lane v Spurs.

City finish 3rd in Division Two. With Mr Cyril Spiers in the management chair, City narrowly miss promotion to the top league. Manchester City and Preston are two points and seven points ahead of them respectively. Trevor Ford scores for Wales in a 3-2 win v the Rest of the UK played at the Cardiff ground in December 1951.

Cup competitions: 15 goals recorded in total over early rounds of the Welsh Cup against Barry Town and Bangor City.

The Bluebirds reach the final but beaten by Merthyr Tydfil. West Ham United put the City out of the FA Cup in January.

Best result: 5-2 thrashing of Grimsby Town in league match. Wilf Grant collects a hat trick and concludes the season as top scorer. Worst result is 4-0 away stinging at Brentford.

Attendances: 30,000 at Upton Park to see City defeated 2-1 v West Ham United in the FA Cup. Highest home attendance finds 37,000 watching a 2-0 victory v Notts County in the Bluebirds' first home match.

CARDIFF CITY

As City's first professional, Jack Evans also had a job as a labourer as well, and worked on the construction of the first wooden stand erected at Ninian Park. His shot was so hard that during a penalty attempt, the force of his strike was such that it broke the wrist of the 'keeper.

season 1951/ 52

City promoted to Division One, as runners-up. With little appearance of Christmas spirit, City play Swansea away on Christmas day with a resulting 1-1 draw outcome. Boxing Day saw the return fixture attended by 46,000 at Ninian Park with Cardiff running out winners by 3-0.
Cup competitions: ko'd early in all.
Best result: 4-0 v Leicester City on the opening day of the season. Wilf Grant nets twice, eventually nabbing 29 over the season. Defeat is not avoided, with Sheffield United smacking City 6-1 at their place.
Attendances: an average of 28,000 regularly attend Ninian Park. More than 52,000 see Leeds United beaten in the 42nd and final match of the season.

season 1952/ 53

City peak at 12th position in Division One. Life in the top division does not prove a walk over for the Bluebirds and they actually lose more games than they win.
Winners of 14 games out of a total of 42, it's a half-dozen less than in their previous promotion-winning season.
Cup competitions: reach semis of the Welsh Cup before a 1-0 defeat by Rhyl calls time. Beaten 3-1 by Halifax Town in the FA Cup.
Best result: 6-0 drubbing of Man City following on from a run of 8 games without a win.
Attendances: 57,893 see Arsenal goal-less draw at Ninian Park. Nearly 60,000 at Highbury to see City come away with a 1-0 win.

season 1953/ 54

City finish 10th position, collecting four additional points this season than over the course of the last one.
Trevor Ford signs for the Bluebirds for a club record fee of £30,000. Cardiff are beaten 3-0 by Arsenal and 6-1 by Manchester United & West Brom in consecutive matches. Bluebird Trevor Ford plays in the Wales side beaten 1-0 by Scotland at Ninian Park in October. Cyril Spiers resigns as manager in May 1954.
Cup competitions: no success in either.
Best result: 5-0 v Charlton with a Ken Chisholm hat trick seen by 50,000 at Ninian Park.

Above badges: Manchester City, West Ham, Notts County, Manchester United, West Brom, Halifax

When former Bluebird John Toshack was a Liverpool player, he used to present a weekly radio show with then-Everton striker Duncan Mackenzie, the latter scored the winning goal against City in a 1-2, 1976/ 1977 season FA Cup tie at Ninian Park.

season 1954/ 55

City finish 20th in Division One.
Cardiff becomes acknowledged as a City whilst a 3rd class return train ticket to London Paddington costs 19 shillings. City mentors Fred stewart and Bart Wilson both pass away. Secretary-manager Trevor Morris is in charge of affairs at Ninian Park and striker Wilf Grant is sold in October. The team avoid relegation by the skin of their teeth, losing 18 matches in all.
Cup competitions: Nothing. Despite Trevor Ford being on target four times in the Welsh Cup. Gerry Hichens is a new arrival at the club and scores on his home debut against League Champions Wolves.
Best result: 3-2 against Wolves at Ninian Park in the penultimate game of the season.
A 12:3 goal ratio in favour of the Bluebirds is recorded against Preston NE, home and away.
Attendances: 39,060 see the City v Wolves match at Ninian Park. A massive 54,000 are at Goodison Park to see City v Everton.

season 1955/ 56

City finish 17th in Division One.
A tough season in the new division for the Bluebirds.
Wolves annihilate them 9-1 in Cardiff in what was only the fifth match of the season. However, in the away fixture it is a different story. Boys Own stuff comes true for Neil O'Halloran as he pops in a hat-trick on his home debut v Charlton. A crowd of 23,000 see the part-timer make his mark in a side with another new arrival, Danny Malloy, signed from Dundee. The season became Alf Sherwood's last in a City shirt.
Cup competitions: City win the Welsh Cup for the first time in twenty-six years, beating Swansea Town 3-2 in front of 37,000 at Ninian Park. The Bluebirds score 23 goals on the way to the final. K.o'd of the FA Cup once more, by West Ham.
Best result: 2-0 defeat of the mighty Wolves at Molineux after the Ninian Park match previously saw City slaughtered 1-9.
Attendances: 44,000 at Manchester United's Old Trafford for City's 1-1 visit in March.

cardiff city 1980

season 1956 / 57

City are relegated to Division Two having gathered a paltry 29 league points.
Cardiff win a meagre 10 games all season, losing 23. Gerry Hitchens nets a marvellous 24 goals for the team in what transpires to be the highest club total in more than 30 years. No wins for the Bluebirds in last 6 games of a dire season. Beaten 6-0 and 6-2 at Preston and Burnley respectively. Trevor Ford and John Charles, both Cardiff players at some time, score a goal each in a 2-2 draw with Scotland at Ninian Park in October.
Cup competitions: No success.
Best result: 5-2 win against Newcastle in the first game of the season played at Ninian Park. Plus a 5-1 squashing of Bristol City on New Year's Eve.
Attendances: 42,000 see City beat the Magpies

season 1957 / 58

City finish 15th in Division Two.
Gerry Hitchens is transferred to Aston Villa and Derek Tapscott is signed from Arsenal. Derek was a full Welsh international at the time.
Best result: Barnsley mashed 7-0 at Ninian Park in December by a splendid Cliff Nugent hat-trick. Nugent was to spend seven years at City. Leeds United defeated 4-1 in the October. Liverpool, the league-leaders pushed aside 6-1 again at Ninian, 30,000 see it. Another hat trick by City player Ron Hewitt at home in a 4-3 win against Blackburn Rovers.
Cup competitions: no joy despite reaching the 5th round of the FA Cup.
Attendances: 45,000 see City's goal-less draw at home for their opening match. Whilst 45,580 are at Ninian to see a goal-less draw with Blackburn Rovers in an FA Cup tie in February. However, league attendances in decline this season, lowest at 7,954 see City lose 3-1 away to Rotherham. 30,000 see City put one over on Leeds at Elland road, 1-2 in the FA Cup.

opposite:
Barnsley, Liverpool and Rotherham United team badges

season 1958/ 59

City finish 9th in Division Two and continue to improve. Derek Tapscott soon reaches double figures in goals scored. Bill Jones becomes City manager and given positioned officially in mid-September superseding the departed Trevor Morris, who leaves for Swansea in July.
Cup competitions: City winners of the Welsh Cup defeating Lovell's Athletic 2-0. No FA Cup joy following a 4th round exit provided by Norwich.
Attendances: 25,000 and 26,000 are at Ninian Park for the visits of Liverpool & Swansea respectively.

Husbands
Mackenzie Duffy
Lawrie Ramsay McDougall
McDonald Abley Malloch Watt Evans

Cardiff City FC's line-up for their first friendly fixture v Aston Villa, 1/ 09/1910.

season 1959/ 60

City finish runners-up in Division Two. The Bluebirds attain promotion to Division One after winning 23 of their 43 matches. Aston Villa took the league title with one point more than City although Graham Moore scores the winner against them in April to take the Bluebirds up.
City manager Bill Jennings sends out a reserve team for a Welsh Cup fixture that clashed with an important league tie v Orient for the Division Two-seeking Bluebirds. Consequently the club was heavily fined by the FAW. City win the Welsh Cup for the 9th time. Derek Tapscott puts in a hat-trick performance during a summer tour of Scandinavia and strikes 20 times over the season.
Cardiff-born lad Colin Baker makes his full debut on Easter Saturday in a City team that ran out 1-0 winners v Aston Villa.
The result meant that the Bluebirds had won promotion.
Cup competitions: Nothing in the FA Cup and lose in the Welsh Cup Final replay at Wrexham after winning it the season before.
Attendances: 52,364 watch City on their way up as they defeat eventual champions Aston Villa in the forth from last game of the season.
Best result: City begin the campaign well with home wins against Liverpool & Middlesborough.

Swansea beaten three times with ex-City man Trevor Morris in charge there. 6-2 win at home v Lincoln City. Bluebirds also put 5 past Charlton & Leyton Orient.

The Bluebirds finish 15th in Division One. 'A great player...great pace and could score a goal.' Former Swans and Newport boss Colin Addison talking about Derek Tapscott, 2004. City now under the management of Bill Jennings and complete the double over eventual League Champions Burnley. Derek 'Tappy' Tapscott pops in a hat trick v W.B.A at Ninian Park in December. In all, Tappy nets 29 goals that season. Floodlights are installed at Ninian Park for the first time. A programme costs 4d.
Cup competitions: City put out their full first-team in Welsh Cup following being fined by the FAW for fielding reserves in the season before. Consequently, City annihilate Knighton 16-0 in a 1st Round tie. Tapscott netted a half-dozen and Moore struck 4! Unfortunately, City would be ko'd in the semis by Swansea.
No luck in the FA Cup.
Best result: future City management disaster Alan Durban scores superfluous goal in 6-1 drubbing at Chelsea's Stamford Bridge.
Attendances: 45,938 [or was it 58,000] are at

Ninian Park for a 3-2 City win v Tottenham Hotspur in March 1961. Whatever the exact attendance that day, it was a great result as Spurs were League and FA Cup winners of the 1960/ 1961 season.

City finish in 21st spot on 32 points [only 5 points less than last season] and are consequentially relegated to Division Two. Mel Charles makes his City debut v Manchester City in February '62. Mel would play on for a further decade before retiring from professional football in the 1971/ 1972 season. Former City hot shot Trevor Ford signs for Newport County but his time with the Ironsides turns out to be brief.
Cup competitions: 3rd round defeats provided by Bournemouth and Middlesborough in the League and FA Cup tournaments.
Best result: a 5 [6] - 2 home victory in the league v Chelsea in the 6th game of the season. City go 3 matches without loss.
Attendances: 61,566 see Wales v England.

season 1962/ 63

Cardiff finish 10th in Division Two.
13 Jan 1962 City v Spurs - with the formidable goal scorer Jimmy Greaves turning out for the visitors in a 1-1 draw watched by 34,020 spectators. Summer '62 : former Swansea Town favourite Ivor Allchurch arrives at City, from Newcastle United, for a fee of £20,000.
Cup competitions: More 3rd round beatings once again.
Best result: 5-2 v Swansea in September.
Attendances: 27,569 see a stupendous 4-4 draw with Newcastle United at Ninian Park.

season 1963/ 64

City are playing in Division Two and finish 15th.
'One does not know what the season holds...but all at Ninian Park are full of confidence and our aim is promotion.' Bold words indeed from the programme notes for the opening game of the season but by December the Bluebirds were 8th from bottom and the Swans 4th from bottom. A cavalcade of

6 defeats at the end of the year overwhelms. John Charles is warmly welcomed as a new Bluebird in his home debut v Norwich City in August and former Wrexham keeper Kevin Keelan makes his debut for the Canaries. The match contains a curious goal from Charles in a 3-1 victory. A teen-aged John Toshack enjoys training with the veteran Charles prior to breaking in to the first team squad. The youngster scored in the next game of the season in front of a crowd of 25,352. The Press box cited in the Bob Bank area, is later to become Radio Ninian. Seats in the ground ranged from 6/6 for the Canton stand and 10/6 in the Grandstand.
Cup competitions: Wrexham put City out of the League Cup by 3-0. Leeds are victorious in the FA Cup by 1-0.
Best result: 5-0 away roasting of Portsmouth.
Attendances: 22,098 see John Charles making his full Cardiff City debut alongside the established likes of Ivor Allchurch, Peter King [pictured below right] and John's own brother, Mel. Whilst 22,000 see a league derby match with Swansea at Ninian Park end in a 1-1 draw.

season 1964/ 65

Cardiff finish 13th in Division Two.

'He didn't have any favourites, and if you didn't do your job for him, he'd soon let you know.' So said former City player Bobby Woodruff who played under the latest Cardiff boss Jimmy Scoular from 1965. Scoular takes charge of the Bluebirds from this season onwards where a City programme sets fans back 6d. Gates at Ninian are down and 'Gentle giant' John Charles makes his final appearance for City in a European match v Standard Liege. With an unlucky 13 games played Cardiff are firmly planted at the bottom of the table. A double 'trouncing' for Swansea Town both at their ground 2-3 by the Bluebirds and 5-0 at Ninian Park with goals from Ivor Allchurch [3] and John Charles[2].

Cup competitions: The Bluebirds win the Welsh Cup beating Bangor City. Cardiff do exceedingly well to make it through to the Quarter finals of the ECWC in their first European adventure. Southampton and Charlton prevent progress in the other cups.

Best results: 6-1 v Middlesborough at home in January, with a Peter King hat trick.

Attendances: 38,458 attend the City v Real Zaragoza match at Ninian Park in February 1965. City are defeated 0-1.

season 1965/ 66

Cardiff finish the season 3rd from bottom.

'For our initial game we entertain the small but famous Lancashire club, Bury.'

No worries for the Bluebirds at the start of the new Division Two campaign as they see off their visitors 1-0 with a John Charles goal. Bury had been battered by 4-0 in the previous season by City. Future boss and former player at City, Alan Durban, returns to play for Derby County who are defeated 2-1. Durban was a prolific marksman for the rams, hitting 23 goals for them in the season before. Some heavy defeats are inflicted upon the Bluebirds; 6-1 by Portsmouth, 5-3 by Southampton and 5-2 by West Ham United in a season from which Cardiff narrowly avoid relegation to Division Three by a solitary point. However, the worst result occurs in the final game of the season, an away fixture at Preston, which City are defeated 9-0. The season saw only 1 substitute allowed to be selected by each team.

Cup competitions: Welsh Cup semi-final defeat by Swansea with Ivor Allchurch in their team,

which won 5-3. West Ham United and Southport put an end to progress in the other cup competitions.
Best result: 5-3 v a later-relegated Middlesborough at Ninian Park and a 4-6 away victory at Rotherham United in August '65.
Attendances:14,768 watch the 5-3 defeat with Southampton.

City again end the season in 20th position: exactly the same as they were last season.
'If we can continue to produce this type of fluid, purposeful play there can be little cause for complaint.'
This early declaration was made when City had won one game and lost two in the onset of the new Division Two season. With a population of 250,000 the City of Cardiff was blossoming but on field, success was not. During his early days with the Bluebirds, John Toshack was nicknamed 'shack' and in this season he scored and missed penalties for the club. Alan Durban once more makes his name known as the former City man scores in a 1-1 draw for Norwich at Ninian Park. Cardiff again narrowly beat the drop finishing 20th out of 22.
Cup competitions: Swansea Town 0 v Cardiff City 5. Cardiff beat the Swans in the 5th round of the Welsh Cup on their way to taking the trophy. Wrexham are defeated in the final.

season 1966/ 67

Early defeats in the League and FA Cup.
Best result: 6-3 v Hereford United in the Welsh Cup. John Charles is player/manager for the visitors that day in February '67.
Attendances: 37,205 for an FA Cup 4th round tie in February.

season 1967/ 68

City finish 13th in the league. 'It was like a dream come true.' Richie Morgan, reflecting upon his debut v Moscow Torpedo. The first 8 out of 12 matches are staged at Ninian Park this campaign that transpires as a rather odd one. City's record of only one loss in the last 17 games played at home is ended by Derby County in a 1-5 defeat. A healthy 17,343 attend the opening match v Plymouth, a resulting 1-1 draw. John Toshack is given an opportunity in Cardiff's European forays and scores v Shamrock Rovers. The visitors are managed by Liam Tuohy, an ex-team mate of present City boss Jimmy Scoular.
Cup competitions: ECWC sees City pitted against Moscow Torpedo, with a team full of Russian international players. Stunningly, City reach the semi-finals where the German side Hamburg eventually knock them out. Cardiff beat a John Charles-led Hereford United 4 -1. Big John gets their strike. Stoke City beat

Cardiff in the 3rd round of the FA Cup and Burnley win 2-1 in a League Cup tie.
Best result: 8-0 v Ebbw Vale with 2 hat tricks, one for Toshack and the other from Peter King. Also, a 3-0 league win v Aston Villa.
Attendances: 43,070 see Hamburg SV at Ninian in the ECWC whilst a further 30,567 see the quarter-final v Moscow Torpedo which City win 1-0. 18,195 see the Aston Villa match at Ninian Park, which sees 3 players carried off, one City and one Villa playing breaking their leg respectively!

above:
Hamburg's unusual team badge and City's own Leighton Phillips as a Wales player

season
1968/69

'A season of achievement.' The Bluebirds finish 5th out of 22 in Division Two. John Toshack is cracking the goals in for City this season, netting twice in the Welsh Cup Final. The result is marred by altercations in the Bob Bank back when rival supporters were not stringently segregated. Tannoy announcements articulate the crowd control concerns. Whilst future City manager Richie Morgan makes his playing debut as a replacement for Don Murray in a European Cup Winners' Cup tie. Leighton Phillips is the first ever City substitute to be used in a European match. John Toshack and Brian Clark are the top Division Two hit men during the season. Although City man Baker retires at the end of the campaign.
Inconsistency is mixed with some good results thereafter: no wins in 9 games from October to December and 3 defeats in the first three games.
Cup competitions: City win the Welsh Cup 5-1 on aggregate over two ties v Swansea. Cardiff do themselves proud by reaching the semi-final of the European Cup Winners' Cup. Arsenal put them out of the FA Cup with a 2-0 triumph.
Best result: 5-0 v Oxford United at Ninian Park.
Attendances: 26,234 see the visit by Bristol City in January.

Cardiff finish 7th in the league with 94 goals scored.

'The verdict was unanimous - a truly great game.' So declared the City programme notes in summarizing the recent City 1 v Leicester City 1 match at Ninian Park. In goal for the visitors that day was Peter Shilton. Swansea Town change their name to Swansea City in December 1969. The cost of a City programme is now one shilling. After a great start with 2 strikes in the first opening games of the season, John Toshack subsequently leaves the club for the glamour of Anfield but offers the City faithful a farewell hat-trick [he did the same in a league match v Q.P.R] v Hull City in October. Cardiff won the match handsomely by 5-1 with 21,837 there to bid him adieu. Violence between City fans and Turkish fans from Goeztepe Izmir after a 1-0 win at Ninian.

Cup competitions: Brian Clarke helps sink the lowly Barmouth and Dyffrin by netting five goals in a Welsh Cup fixture. They march on to win the final v Chester. Out in the 2nd round of the ECWC. No joys in either the FA or League cup tournaments.

Best result: 7-1 v Mjondalen I.F, a Second Division Norwegian side. Toshack and Clark crack in a brace each. In the home leg, Sandy Allan strikes a hat-trick in a 5-1 win. Attendances: 27, 932 attend the first home game of the season to see the visit of Swindon Town. Future City manager Frank Burrows is in their side that draw with Cardiff 2-2. The biggest home gate proves to be just over 30k for a 4-2 win v Q.P.R.

'The magic moment.' City's 1-0 defeat of Real Madrid at Ninian Park, March, 1971.

Cardiff finish the season in a commendable 3rd in Division Two. A Bluebirds ballpoint pen could be bought for 9d and a holdall for £1 10 shillings in the club shop this season. Cardiff, twinned with Nantes in France, show no special discompensation when the two footballing sides meet in the ECWC; City running out 7-2 aggregate winners. Mighty John Toshack chalked up his 100th goal for Cardiff this season. His successor, a 21-year-old called Alan Warboys, scores twice on his home debut v Sheffield Wednesday. Cardiff play their 40th competitive fixture v Bristol City in March '71.

Cup competitions: Cardiff win the Welsh Cup and thus play in Europe for the 4th season.

Best result: 8-0 thrashing of P.O Larnaca in September 1970 in the European Cup Winners' Cup. The true winner being an amazing 1-0 defeat of Real Madrid in a European tie. Attendances: 47,500 are at Ninian Park for the Real Madrid tie on 10 March '71. Whilst 21,865 see a fine Toshack hat trick in the league v Hull City in October.

City finish a disappointing 19th in Division Two, some 19 points down on the previous season.

'This is the Big One.'
Cardiff entertain Leeds United in February and are soundly beaten 2-0.
Cardiff are once more playing in Europe and the Ninian Park grass is replaced in readiness. A season ticket this year costs £11 for the Grandstand area. Meanwhile on the pitch, Phil Dwyer scores his first City goal v Preston, via a header, in October. The Bluebirds spend most of their season at the bottom of the table up until December.
Former City favourite John Charles becomes player-manager with Merthyr Tydfil in January '72 and soon returns to Ninian Park in an unfamiliar but welcome guise.
Cup competitions: City in the European Cup Winners' Cup knocked-out by Dynamo Berlin. The potent Leeds with Johnny Giles, Alan Clarke et al beat City 2-0 in a Fifth round FA Cup game at Ninian Park. Perpetual irritants

West Ham defeat Cardiff in a 2nd round League Cup replay fixture. Jimmy Andrews is assistant manager with fellow Division Two side Luton.
Best result: 6-1 victory v Charlton in October. Attendances: the FA Cup tie with Leeds is watched by an amazing 49,180. The visit by West Ham United sees 30,109 to see a team including Geoff Hurst and Trevor Brooking. The Hammers take home a 2-1 win.

Superstitions: City Striker Tony Evans always carried a ball onto the pitch prior to kick off.

City finish 20th in Division Two.
A winger called Gil Reece arrives at Ninian Park from Sheffield United in an exchange deal that saw City scorer Alan Warboys head up North. Also signing on for the Bluebirds in October was Willie Anderson, signed from Aston Villa for £65,000. Future City star Robbie James makes his league debut aged sixteen for Swansea City. He will stay with the Swans for a decade and arrives at Ninian Park for the 1992/93 season. Cup competitions: progress stalls in a 4th round replay loss at Bolton Wanderers in the FA Cup. Bristol Rovers pummel City 3-1 in the League Cup.
Best result: Bangor City beaten 5-0 by Cardiff in the Welsh Cup Final.

Attendances: 21,982 are at Ninian Park to see a 1-1 draw with Sunderland in the penultimate game of the season.

City close the season in 17th position. Jimmy Scoular leaves the City helm after 9 years in November and former Manchester United boss Frank O'Farrell briefly comes in. He in turn leaves the City in the lurch for a coaching position in the round-ball oasis that is Iran. His assistant, Jimmy Andrews is left to take control for the remaining part of the campaign. The Bluebirds struggle in the league and require a point v Crystal Palace to stay up: they scrape a 1-1 draw and send Palace down. The main grandstand at Ninian Park is extended and club programme set you back 7p. Ex-Bluebird Ivor Allchurch is still playing football now with Haverfordwest.

Cup competitions: Success in winning the Welsh Cup. Meet Sporting Lisbon in the European Cup Winners' Cup and hold them to a 0-0 draw at Ninian Park but go out 2-1 in front of 50,000 at their Estadio Jose Alvalade. Progress in the home cup tournaments is made redundant by defeats by Birmingham City and Burnley.
Best result: 5-0 defeat of Oxford United in September.

Attendances: 27,139 spectators watch a 1-1 draw with Crystal Palace at Ninian Park in what was the final game of the season.

City are relegated following a tally of 32 points leaving them in 21st position. Don Murray is off on a brief loan to Swansea who put in a poor display in Division Four too. A sad tally of 36 goals is all that the Bluebirds manage to score all season. Leighton Phillips is sold to Aston Villa.
Cup competitions: Lose the Welsh Cup final. Soundly beaten in the 1st round of the ECWC by Hungarian side Ferecvaros. Leeds United beat City 4-1 in the FA Cup and Bristol City do likewise in the League Cup by 2-1.
Best result: 4-0 win in the Welsh Cup v Oswestry Town. Attendances: 4,228 European tie v Ferecvaros.

City runners-up in Division Three and promoted back to Division Two. 'Adrian was a big lad with great vision and an ability to do the unexpected.' 21 year old City forward Tony Evans speaking about his then new striking partner Adrian Alston. New faces in the form of Doug Livermore and Alston arrive at the club whilst old ones such as Gill Reece depart. Brian Clark returns to once again play as a Bluebird during the summer of 1975 after plying his trade away from Wales for the previous three years. After being relegated the previous season Cardiff go straight back up. Veteran Mike England, whom had only arrived at the start of the season, plays his final game for City in the 1-0 win at Bury which clinches promotion. Shrewsbury Town, then managed by player-boss Alan Durban come to Cardiff and are sent home with their tails between their legs following a 3-0 spanking! Having earlier played out a thrilling 4-4 draw at their Eastville ground, with Evans hitting all of the City goals, the blue side of Bristol, Rovers, remove Cardiff in the League Cup whilst Southend put in a 2-0 win in the 4th round of the FA Cup.

Cup competitions: City beat Hereford in a re-played Welsh Cup final. Striker Tony Evans hit a hat trick on the way to the final and scored in both legs of the said Hereford ties. After a sluggish start he notches up a total of 29 goals that season.

Best result: 5-2 v Peterborough United.

Attendances: 35,000+ see City beat the actual league champions Hereford United.

season 1976/77

Division 2
Carlisle United
SATURDAY, MAY 14, 1977
Kick Off 3 p.m.

Cardiff, playing in Division Two, finish 18th out of 22. '...a fabulous sight at the end of the Wrexham game. It seemed to us...that the entire crowd was erupting in our mutual triumph...' City player Doug Livermore speaking after an FA Cup win over Wrexham, January '77. City's first three games are v Bristol Rovers and local lad David Giles makes his City debut v Hereford United, scoring a goal. A total of 36 arrests were recorded following the FA Cup match v Tottenham Hotspur in January 1977, the severity of which was described by local police as 'pretty bad'. City enigma Robin Friday suffers a fractured cheekbone against Charlton after arriving at Ninian Park some twenty minutes prior to kick-off. Friday shines on his debut against the 1975 FA Cup winners Fulham, scoring two of the three goals in a 3-1 win watched by 20,268 (City also win the away match too). The attendance at Ninian Park had increased in the hope of seeing both George Best and Rodney Marsh play on a bitterly cold afternoon: neither did. However, Best apologized in the press for not turning out that day. Former England World Cup winning captain Bobby Moore was playing for the visitors and was run ragged by the new pretender who rattled him by repeatedly squeezing a certain part of his anatomy! Upon signing for City, it was arranged that Friday would be met at Cardiff's train station; a phone call was received at the club stating that he had been arrested for only having a platform ticket for his trip down from Reading! Late on, Cardiff failed to produce a win in 7 games and avoided relegation by a single point. A City programme had a cover price of 10p.

Cup competitions: "It's one of those games you can look at and say 'anything can happen and probably will." So offered Jimmy Andrews upon learning that Cardiff had drawn an FA Cup home tie v Spurs.

City beat them 1-0 with a magical Peter Sayer goal on 8th January 1977. The Bluebirds had taken care of Welsh counterparts Wrexham in the last round. Everton were their next opponents at Ninian Park in February and defeat City 1-2. Russian side Dynamo Tiblisi provide an early exit from the ECWC.

Best result: that 1-0 win v Spurs in the cup and a 1-1 home draw v Carlisle that saved City from relegation in May 1977. A good 1-4 away win at table-toppers Wolves is attained in front of 21,234 in April.

Attendances: 27,868 are there to see the giant-killing FA Cup tie followed by an even mightier 35,953 who fill Ninian Park to see the visit of Division One big boys Everton. 80,000 see the City away tie v Dynamo Tbilisi in the September.

top left:
David Giles,
Peter Sayer,
Spurs kit &
former Brighton
defender
Mark Lawrenson

season 1977 / 78

Cardiff City

(Blue with Yellow, White stripe)

1 Ron HEALEY
2 Phil DWYER
3 Freddie PETHARD
4 Alan CAMPBELL
5 Paul WENT
6 Albert LARMOUR
7 Doug LIVERMORE
8 Peter SAYER

City avoid relegation by one point. Robin Friday heads in a goal from a corner to secure a point for Cardiff in a 1-1 draw played two days before the Welsh Cup final. The season belongs to Mr Friday after he scores twice in a home win against Luton Town in April '77. The game played out a one-to-one battle between Luton goalie Milija Aleksic and the aforementioned Robin F. The Cardiff boy won the day and stuck up two fingers to the floored Aleksic, an image captured for posterity by Echo photographer David Jones. Consequently, he was suspended for the next two games in spite of the fact that the referee missed the gesture! The footballing legend that is George Best played for Fulham at Ninian Park during the season too. However, the Cottagers went home empty-handed following a 3-1 spanking. In an away game at Brighton's old Goldstone ground Friday is sent off and after being chastised by City boss Jimmy Andrews, he throws his team mates clothes into the baths of the changing rooms. Cup competitions: Welsh Cup final losers to Shrewsbury Town. City battle in the European Cup Winners' Cup even though they lost in the Welsh Cup Final: they flop in the 1st round.

Best result: 5-2 win at Ninian Park v Sunderland and conversely, City thumped 6-1 at Bolton and 6-2 at Sheffield United. Attendances: only 3,631 attend the goal less Euro tie v FK Austria Memphis. Southampton, with World Cup '66 winner Alan Ball, are beaten 1-0 in front of 11,359 at Ninian Park.

season 1978 / 79

'What a season of mixed fortunes this has been!' Bob Grogan, City chairman, May 1978. The Bluebirds finish the season in 9th position with only 4 more points collected than from last season but climbing 10 places higher. The Safety of Sports ground Bill 1977 resulted in Cardiff City FC being refused a safety certificate by the local council. The Grange End stand was demolished as a consequence, despite the club losing 2k a week. Former City hero John Toshack becomes the Swansea City player-manager in March 1978. Robin Friday is sent off in an away game at Brighton & Hove Albion for retaliating against upcoming BBC sports pundit Mark Lawrenson. City lost 4-0 and Friday was banned for the next two fixtures. In his career, the City striker was booked 20 times. He left the club in December 1977. George Best plays v City at Ninian Park in a downtrodden Fulham side that are well beaten, 3-1. Late November into early December finds the Bluebirds losing

three games and conceding 14 goals in the process. 'One of the most difficult seasons any club could have experienced.' So said City Paul Went, who score v Notts County in the penultimate game of the season that saved the Bluebirds from relegation. Admission prices for OAP's and children are halved to 50p. A new name is announced as manager at Cardiff City in November '78: one Richie Morgan. Constantinous 'Tarki' Micellef, an ex-apprentice and local lad, makes his full Cardiff debut in a Second Division match v Sheffield United. He stayed with the club until 1983. A programme featuring a distinctive blue with yellow/white strip, just like the City kit, is sold on match days at 15p. New arrival Gary Stevens finishes the season as joint top scorer by netting in 5 successive matches as the season begins. He also pops in a hat trick in a friendly against Minehead. Also of note is the fixture against Leyton Orient in February '79 sees debuts for Linden Jones and Ronnie Moore.

Best result: 4-0 v Sheffield United with a hat trick from John Buchanan. Attendances: 14,851 are at Ninian Park to see Stoke City take the points with a 3-1 win.

City conclude the season in15th place in Division Two. A programme for the City home fixtures costs 20p for this season. Ex-City captain Doug Livermore returned to City as a

member of the coaching staff at Ninian Park. Concluding a fourteen-year gap, league matches recommence against Swansea City. The Swans draw first blood at the Vetch Field but lose at Ninian Park in a 1-0 April return. Wales also beat England 4-1 at the Racecourse. Cup competitions: FA Cup 3rd round tie v Arsenal at Ninian Park sees the Bluebirds hold the Gunners to a goal-less draw. The visiting side with the likes of Pat Jennings and Willie Young amongst their ranks defeat City in the 3-1 replay in north London. A programme for that home match cost 50p. Swansea City beat Cardiff in the Welsh Cup 6th round at the Vetch Field and their scorers included ex-City stars David Giles and John Toshack. Along with another former City star, Leighton Phillips, they come to Ninian Park in January for an FA Cup 3rd round replay. Yet another past City name, Tony Evans, turns out for a 2-1 winning Birmingham City side at Ninian Park also.
Best result: John Buchanan scores 8 times in a friendly v Rhayader.
Attendances: 16,328 for the 1-2 home defeat by a strong Chelsea.

Cardiff beat relegation from Division Two by a single point ending in 19th place.'I am a manager who believes in flair.' City boss Richie Morgan.City administer a 3-3 draw with

Swansea City on 27 December with City boy John Buchanan scoring a cracking goal from some 35+ yards out. The upper-lipped haired Peter Kitchen signs for City from Fulham in August '80 for £100,000. Manchester City man Tony Brook came to City in November 1980 to assist with coaching matters. Additional City/Swansea tussles saw a 1-1 draw at the Vetch Field in April '81. The Swans won promotion to the top flight at the conclusion of the campaign. A programme at City now cost 30p.
Cup competitions: Cardiff reach the Welsh Cup Final where they meet the John Toshack-moulded Swansea City. The hooligan element is endemic at both clubs during this period.
Best result: Peter Kitchen scores 5 in a 6-0 Welsh Cup whitewash of Cardiff Corinthians.
Attendances: poor for this 'nightmare' of a season as described by Morgan.

Cardiff are relegated to Division Three. 'It is very important that everyone remains nice and cool.' So recommended the new City head-honcho Len Ashurst shortly before Cardiff's final game of the season against Luton Town. Before this, City boss Ritchie Morgan had moved to backroom duties to be replaced by former West Brom and Wales international Graham Williams. Some four months later finds City losing 9 of their 11 games played. Len

Ashurst arrives in March '82 but cannot halt the slide and City lose 2-3 in the last league game of the season. The team that beat them are the division champions Luton Town. Roger Gibbins comes to City on a free transfer but does not make his full debut until the oncoming season. Both Cardiff and Wrexham are relegated this season whilst Swansea climb and finish a marvellous sixth in the giddy heights of the old Division One. Hooliganism in the crowd at the Welsh Cup Final derby between Cardiff and Swansea mars the latter's victory at the Vetch. Ron Healey calls it a day as one of Cardiff's best-loved keepers. Ex-City skipper Billy Ronson returns to his old club in his new Rotherham colours as does David Giles for Crystal Palace (City lost 1-0).

Cup competitions: Swansea retain the Welsh Cup by beating Cardiff 2-1 in the 2nd leg of the final in May. Years later, Gary Bennett informs the author that this was the one regret of his career with the Bluebirds, not winning the final that season.

Best result: 4-1 victory v Wrexham in round 5 of the Welsh Cup.

Attendances: 11,960 for the Welsh Cup final game v Swansea City. Attendances a lot higher away with an average of 7,000 at Ninian Park.

City players first wore numbers on their shirts during the aborted 1939/ 40 season.

season 1982/ 83

Cardiff finish runners-up in Division Three on 86 points. 'A down to earth northern bloke from Sunderland. Honest and genuine.' Paul Bodin re: City boss Len Ashurst, interviewed in the Thin Blue Line fanzine Issue 59 [2004].'It's the Bennett double act. Goals and excitement from Dave and Gary.' The Mancunian Bennett brothers star in the City side this season with Dave arriving as an established name whilst Gary makes his way to first team prominence from the reserves. Both score a goal apiece in games v Millwall and Walsall at Ninian Park. City go up back up to Division Two but both Wrexham and Swansea are relegated. Fabulously enough, the Bluebirds lose only one game at home all season and clinch promotion after a 2-0 Ninian Park defeat of Leyton Orient on 7 May '83. Veteran striker Bob Hatton arrives at City, his ninth club, to bolster the attack. He proves a great success. Future City name Nigel Vaughan plays for Newport County at Ninian Park this season in a December fixture attended by 15,972. Cardiff lose one match at home throughout the season.

Cup competitions: a hugely embarrassing 2-3 FA Cup defeat to the hands of Weymouth in December '82 weighs heavily on the mind of manager Len Ashurst. 'Pure farce.' Is his definition of the winning goal in that eventful match, '[City defender] Jimmy Mullen was tying his bootlaces and told [goalkeeper] Dibble to hold on with his goal-kick,' the manager told the SW Echo, 'but Andrew took it and miscued.' A goal followed and Cardiff were out of the FA Cup in the 2nd round. The Bluebirds saw an October visit from Arsenal in the Milk Cup with a 1-3 defeat watched by 11,632.

Best result: 2-0 v Portsmouth with the winner scored by past Pompey star Jeff Hemmerman.

Attendances: 15, 972 see the 3-2 home win over Notts County in December.

'Times are difficult at this club right now.' Len Ashurst, November '83.

Cardiff finish 14th in Division Two. Jimmy Goodfellow becomes Cardiff manager with Jimmy Mullen given the assistant manager/ player role after Ashurst leaves for Sunderland in February '84. Many players follow including Gordon Owen, Andy Dibble and Gary Bennett. Toshack also leaves the recently relegated Swansea City after attaining a fairy tale amount of success for the Vetch Field side culminating in topping the old First Division. The two City sides met for a

Boxing Day game played out at Ninian Park with 14,000+ seeing the Swans take home a 2-3 win; the return game seeing City reverse the result. The coffers being tight, Cardiff City and Newport County completed a five-man exchange in September '83 with Nigel Vaughan and Karl Elsey coming to Ninian Park and Linden Jones, Tarki Micallef and John Lewis off in the opposite direction.

Cup competitions: Ipswich visit in an FA Cup tie with Russell Osman in their side.

Best result: two 5-0 victories v Cambridge United and Taffs Well (seen by only 894 spectators at Ninian Park).

Attendances: 14,580 see the seasonal fixture with Swansea City. It would prove to be the best attended game of the whole season.

City are relegated back down to Division Three after one season spent in the Second. 'We will be doing our utmost to give you an enjoyable day.' The words of Alan Durban printed in his City programme notes in March 1985. The Bluebirds were beaten 4-1 by Notts County at Ninian Park that day, with no wins in the next 4 games being recorded. Durban had replaced Jimmy Goodfellow, who

had been put in temporary charge of team affairs up until the former Cardiff midfielder was announced as the new City boss in October 1984. A total of thirteen players are brought in whilst Phil Dwyer makes his 573rd appearance v Notts County. Dean Saunders plays 4 games for Cardiff whilst on loan from neighbouring Swansea City. Saunders, a veteran full Wales international continues his prolific scoring record for every club that he had played for. The local derby v Swansea City takes place at 11am on a Boxing Day morning at Ninian Park. City take the honours following a 1-0 win. The ground is looking tired and showing its age. On 28 December, City play local rivals Newport County with both Tarki Micalef and Linden Jones both playing against their old club. The match ends in a 1-1 draw. By December, a succession of four defeats and two draws sees City cement their position at the bottom.
Cup competitions: City put out of the Welsh Cup by a 4-0 defeat by Hereford United. Gillingham do the same to them in the FA Cup. Best result: a brace of 3-0 home victories in April v Barnsley and Huddersfield.
Attendances: 6,802 are at Ninian Park when City record a 2-1 win v Leeds United while the 3-0 defeat by Man City is seen by a little over 6000

Opposite: the 1985/ 1986 Cardiff City kit design.

season 1985/ 86

City are relegated to Division Four for the first time. David Giles, a Cardiff name from the 1970s returns to play for City in September '85 having left the club in December '78 and formerly a Newport County player. Another name from the Somerton Park past, Nigel Vaughan, scores the winning goal against Newport in a 2-3 away win. Frank Burrows takes charge of City in May 1986 after Alan Durban is sacked. Swansea inflicts a 4th consecutive defeat in eleven days for Cardiff in a 2-0 win at the Vetch.
Cup competitions: Brian Flynn scores twice as a Bluebird v Swansea in a Milk Cup match with the Swans having veteran 'keeper Jimmy Rimmer as their number one.

season 1986/ 87

City close the season in 13th spot. With Frank Burrows the new City boss in May '86 there is much chopping and changing of the team squad. Ex- Brighton keeper Graham Moseley [above] comes to City on a free transfer as does Alan Curtis from Southampton.

Cup competition: City battle against the Millwall in three FA Cup ties before going out to Stoke City.

Best result: a good 4-0 thrashing of Hartlepool at the end of the season. City come back from 4-1 down to beat the Pilgrims from Plymouth in the League Cup also.

Attendances: 11,505 saw the Boxing Day match with league rivals Swansea City finish goal less. Conversely, a meagre 1,510 see the final game of the season at Ninian Park.

season 1987/ 88

'It was a good blend and there was a great camaraderie inside the dressing room.' City striker Jimmy Gilligan, speaking in the Western Mail. Cardiff City gain promotion from the Barclay's Division Three. The division finds Cardiff competing alongside Swansea, Newport County and Wrexham. The Bluebirds win the Welsh Cup and are automatically entered in the European Cup Winners' Cup despite the UEFA ban on English clubs. A run of 5 wins sees the side go up in style.

Newport are well beaten at Ninian Park by 4-0.

Cup competitions: City take the Welsh Cup v Wrexham and take up a place in Europe.

Best result: Cambridge United are beaten 4-0 at their own ground by the Bluebirds and City crush local rivals Newport County in a Ninian Park fixture seen by 6,536 fans.

Attendances: 10,125 see City beat Crewe and cement promotion.

season 1988/ 89

Cardiff finish 16th in Division Three. The Bluebirds complete a poor season by avoiding relegation by three points. Frank Burrows leave the management hot seat. City fans are allowed admission back in at the Vetch Field following a 5 year ban. Jimmy Gilligan continues to be the club's top scorer with 14 strikes; he nets a hat-trick v Derry Town in a 4-0 tie of the European Cup Winners' Cup.

Cup competitions: After an eleven year hiatus Cardiff compete in their 12th season of European football beating Derry in the first round and losing 6-1 on aggregate to Danish side Aarhus in the next.

Best result: 4-0 v Derry and 4-1 v Enfield in the FA Cup.

Attendances: 10,675 attend a Boxing Day match at Ninian Park with Welsh rivals Swansea

City. The game finishes 2-2 with both City goals coming from Jimmy Gilligan.

season 1989 / 90

Cardiff are relegated To Division Four. A 14-year-old Scott Young signs schoolboy terms with the club.
Hot shot Jimmy Gilligan leaves the Bluebirds to join Portsmouth for a fee of £215,000.
Cup competitions: 50,000+ gate receipts from a goal-less draw with Q.P.R in the FA Cup are stolen from Ninian Park.
Best result: Swansea City are beaten at their own ground on Boxing Day by a single goal. In the next April City lose 0-2 at Ninian Park. Both teams are relegated at the end of the season campaign.
Attendances: 12,244 are at the Vetch to see the Cardiff seasonal win. 13,834 see the draw with Q.P.R.

CARDIFF
CITY

season 1990 / 91

Cardiff finish 13th in the Barclays League. 'No doubt knowing Len Ashurst as I do, we will be in for a very hard game.' Frank Burrows, October 1990. Burrows was then manager at Portsmouth when Pompey eventually beat City in a cup match replay. With glamorous visits from sides such as Scarborough, Mansfield and Torquay in the early part of the campaign optimism is at a low point at Ninian Park. An appalling season for the Bluebirds sees their confidence knocked following an FA Cup replay to Ismian League side Hayes finishing in a 1-0 defeat. Consequently, Cardiff produce no wins in the next 5 games up until a 3-1 home win v Carlisle United. Amazingly, this is reversed by mid-February as the team go on a run of 9 games undefeated. Dire results persist at the end of the campaign; losing 5 and drawing 3 of the last 8 games. In all, the City team scored 43 goals in 46 matches. Len Ashurst quits as manager at the end of the season.
Team-wise, local lad Chris Pike links up well with Guyana-born striker Cohen Griffiths [later to play for Merthyr Tydfil] in the City attack whilst Roger Hansbury is an ever-present in the

keeper's shirt [seen opposite].
Cup competitions: Portsmouth put
out the Bluebirds in a League Cup
replay whilst Merthyr Tydfil beat
Cardiff 1-4 at Ninian Park in the
Welsh Cup. Merthyr where then
playing in the Vauxhall Conference.
Worse was to come in the FA Cup
where the Ishmian League side
Hayes put the Bluebirds out after a
goal-less tie at Ninian Park was concluded by
a 1-0 home win for them. Cardiff were 9th in
Division 4 at the time. A memorable highlight
from that team being former West Brom star
Cyril Regis.
Attendances: 4,805 attend an April Fools Day
match at Ninian Park.

season 1991/92

Cardiff finish 9th in
the Barclays League.
Eddie May becomes
the new Cardiff City
manager in July '91
replacing Len Ashurst in the Ninian Park hot
seat. May had originally been the youth team
coach at City. Cameron, son of John, Toshack
made his debut as a Cardiff City player in
September 1991. Changes at Ninian Park
include a new, extended roof on the
grandstand and seating on the upper-section of
the Bob Bank. Robbie James, former Wales and
Swansea name, comes to the club that season

and is voted Player of the Year as well as Man
of the Match in the Autoglass defeat by
Swansea. Future Cardiff manager Frank Hibbitt
is in charge of Walsall when City play there in
January. As is another City managerial name
Frank Burrows, only this time in charge of
Swansea. Promotion looked an achievable aim
even in January, with City producing a half-
dozen victories, 2 draws and not a single
defeat. Twenty-one year old City striker Chris
Pike nets more than 20 goals for Cardiff during
the course of the season.
Cup competitions: City win the 106th Welsh
Cup in a 5-0 thrashing at the National Stadium,
Swansea are eliminated on the way. However,
Swansea City vanquishes the Bluebirds in an
early round of the FA Cup whilst Bournemouth
also take care of them in the League Cup.
Best result: 5-0 v Wrexham, capped by a hat
trick by local lad Chris Pike.
Attendances: 16,030 see ex-Bluebird Jimmy
Mullen score twice in 0-2 win for eventual
champions Burnley. Mullen was then their
player-manager.

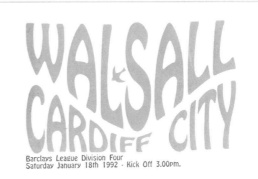

Barclays League Division Four
Saturday January 18th 1992 · Kick Off 3.00pm.

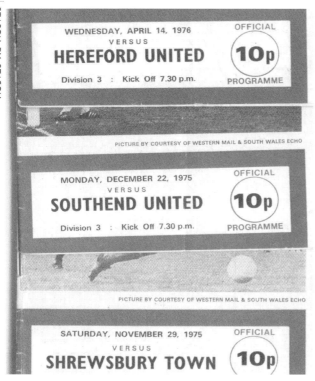

WEDNESDAY, APRIL 14, 1976
VERSUS
HEREFORD UNITED
Division 3 : Kick Off 7.30 p.m.
OFFICIAL
10p
PROGRAMME

PICTURE BY COURTESY OF WESTERN MAIL & SOUTH WALES ECHO

MONDAY, DECEMBER 22, 1975
VERSUS
SOUTHEND UNITED
Division 3 : Kick Off 7.30 p.m.
OFFICIAL
10p
PROGRAMME

PICTURE BY COURTESY OF WESTERN MAIL & SOUTH WALES ECHO

SATURDAY, NOVEMBER 29, 1975
VERSUS
SHREWSBURY TOWN
OFFICIAL
10p

City coach taking the Bluebirds into Europe once more after winning the Welsh Cup. May had enjoyed some 9 matches for Wrexham in the same competitions a number of seasons before. Veteran Robbie James establishes himself in the City side after arriving from Bradford last season. James made his name as a Swansea player but this season he is steadfast in making 42 appearances fro the Bluebirds. Derek Brazil, Paul Ramsey and Carl Dale are all added to the City squad.

Cup competitions: Cardiff face Admira Wacker in the first round of the ECWC and are booted out by a 3-1 aggregate. Bath City embarrass the Bluebirds by winning 3-2 in the 1st round of the FA Cup. Bristol City smash City 6-1 on aggregate in the League Cup tournament.

Best result: 5-0 drubbing of Rhyl in the Welsh Cup Final highlighted by a Phil Stant hat trick. Jason Perry, a City team-mate said of him, 'Stanty was one of the most hard working players I've ever been in a side with.'

season 1992/93

City win the Third Division title. Locally-born Nathan Blake hits a hat-trick v Stockport County in what transpires as his final season at Ninian Park. He pops in a total of 11 goals in the 44 games played that campaign. Eddie May is the

season 1993/94

Cardiff finish 19th in Division Two.
Cup competitions: City meet another City, Manchester City in a televised match with Nathan Blake scoring a smasher. They go out to the Hatters from Luton in the next round with teenaged Billy

Hardy look-a-like John Hartson in their team. Standard Liege prove to be the final European opponents for City this season.
Best result: 4-1 v Swansea City in the semi-final of the Welsh Cup. Unfortunately, Cardiff lose in the final 2-1 to Barry Town.

Attendances: 20,486 see the Manchester City Cup game.

season 1994/ 95

Cardiff are relegated to the Endsleigh League Division Three. Admission to Ninian Park had been increased for the new season that found Terry Yorath as general manager and Eddie May employed as Team boss. Robbie James, having left the Bluebirds, joins Barry Town. Mr Yorath allowed his name to be involved with a consortium that took control of Cardiff City Football Club in 1995 but chaos and misappre-hensions ensued, with Yorath allegedly unaware that they were leasing the club and had not bought it outright, as he was led to believe. Writing in his autobiography, Terry summarizes the period as of nightmarish proportions and proving to be ultimately exasperating.
Cup competition: k.o'd 1-0 in the 1st round of the FA Cup by Enfield. No success elsewhere.
Best result: 7-0 v Ebbw Vale in the Welsh Cup, with a hat trick for Carl Dale. Former Bluebird David Giles is in the visitors team that had held

City to a respectable 1-1 draw at their ground. Attendances: 7,420 watch the City 0 v BirminghamCity 1 match at Ninian Park.

City finish 22nd in Division Three.
Kenny Hibbitt and Phil Neal steer a fragile ship called Cardiff City FC as it hits rocky ground, winning a meagre 11 out of 46 matches all season long. Striker Carl Dale helps City achieve some points by scoring 4 times in the last five matches. He struck a hat-trick v Doncaster Rovers also.
Cup competitions: Matt LeTissier and Southampton come to Wales for a Coca-Cola Cup match, defeat the Bluebirds 5-1 on aggregate. Swindon put City out of the FA Cup.
Attendances: a meagre 3,721 see Cardiff beaten 1-3 by Swansea City in December. The Swans have former Liverpool man Jan Molby appointed as player/manager in February 1996. Billed as the 'new John Toshack' things never pan out as such for the Danish international.

season 1995/ 96

season 1996/ 97

City finish the season 7th in the newly-sponsored Nationwide Division Three.

Cup competition: Gillingham put City out of the FA Cup, Northampton do the same in the League Cup [aka Coca-Cola Cup] and in the Auto Windscreens Shield, Exeter City put an end to progress for the Bluebirds.

Best result: 0-1 away v Swansea City with the winning goal courtesy of 19-year-old striker Simon Haworth. The win put the Bluebirds up in to play-offs contention. Future Cardiff City manager Alan Cork is in charge at the Vetch and he leads his team to a 1-0 victory at home in November.

Attendances: low. 3,721 are at Ninian Park for the Swansea match whilst 4,443 are recorded for the return fixture at the Vetch Field. A ridiculous 793 are at Ninian Park for the Auto Windscreens Cup fixture with Exeter City.

season 1997/ 98

The Bluebirds reside at 21st position in Division Two of the Nationwide League. 'Everybody at Cardiff City Football Club is pulling in the same direction and are all working towards the same common goal.' City manager Russell Osman, speaking during the season when the City was 6 places from the bottom of the division. Osman was manager whilst Kenny Hibbitt was the Director of Football at the club. Frank Burrows was also involved with the club during the season too. Cardiff finished the campaign on 48 points [champions Notts County won the league on 82 points] and only three places from the bottom. The end run in to the season proves disastrous with no wins in their final seven league games. Swansea are beaten 1-0 at Ninian Park and held to a 1-1 at the Vetch.

Cup competitions: beaten by bogey club Reading in the FA Cup, Southend in the Coca-Cola Cup and by Millwall in the Auto Windscreen Shield!

Best result: 1-1 with eventual champions Notts County in August. Also, a 7-1 away trouncing of Doncaster Rovers in the league.

Attendances: 10,174 see the home FA Cup tie v Reading finish 1-1.

season 1998/ 99

City advance on up to Division Two by finishing 3rd in Division Three. In a successful season the Bluebirds gain promotion, making it their ninth such event since joining the football league back in 1910. They end the season in third spot behind Brentford and Cambridge United, respectively. Kevin Nugent knocks in the blue goals whilst future Aston Villa convert Mark Delaney proves consistent in the number 2 shirt for Cardiff. Leo Fortune-West scores a dozen goals for Cardiff in 36 games that he played up front for this City campaign.

Cup competitions: The Blues from Chester City

above: the popular bank aka 'bob bank' seen from the Grandstand on a match day afternoon.

Jimmy Blair: As a City player and full Scottish international captain in the 1920s, after his playing days were over Blair went on to run the Ninian Park pub on Leckwith road. The original has since been demolished.

Writing in the Cardiff Post, the late Bill Barrett, recounted an scene that occurred during a midweek game at Ninian Park against Plymouth Argyle back in the 1950s. Argyle player Moses Russell hopped over the low wall that was once there and bopped a City fan that had been verbally lambasting his challenges. Russell then jumped back over and the game recommenced, all the while the referee had missed the incident and the unfortunate supporter garnered no sympathy from others gathered on the bank.

are demolished 6-0 in the FA Cup 1st round. Best result: 4-2 v the Stags of Mansfield Town. Attendances: 13,000 at Ninian Park on penultimate game of the season. One point from a goal-less draw v Scunthorpe is enough to gain promotion. Attendances prior to this were little under 10,000. Exceptions included 12,452 for a 3-0 home win v Shrewsbury Town on Boxing Day. The Town were then managed by ex-Bluebird player Jake King, a defender with the club in the mid-1980s.

season 1999/00

'Matches against non-league sides are always going to be tough...' Eddie May. Cardiff are relegated to Division Three. Billy Ayre is momentarily appointed manager in the summer 2000 prior to Bobby Gould's tenure after Sam Hamman bought the club. Past member of the Wimbledon 'Crazy Gang, Alan Cork, comes in as head coach a little after and is then given the managerial role.

Cup competitions: no success in any of the English cups but the Welsh Cup final [now known as the F.A.W Premier Cup] is reached by Cardiff only for a 2-0 win for Wrexham.

Best result: Brian Flynn's Wrexham are mashed 5-0 at Ninian Park.

Attendances: 16,030 see the City v Burnley

fixture that the visitors won 2-0. Incredibly, a mid-week away league trip to Scarborough is attended by 935 spectators. Conversely, less than a thousand are at Ninian Park for a 4-1 Welsh Cup win v Caernarfon.

season 2000/ 01

Cardiff gain promotion to Division Three as runners-up to Brighton &H.A.

Alan Cork is the City manager with assistance from former Wales boss Bobby Gould in a successful season that saw Cardiff go up with two games still to play.

Cup competitions: Put out of the FA Cup by Crewe Alexandra.

Best result: 6-1 defeat of Exeter City on New Year's Day.

Attendances: 13,403 are at Ninian Park to watch the 1-1 draw with Crewe.

season 2001/ 02

'The ambitious Welsh club are hoping to gain their second successive promotion... after significantly strengthening their squad...' So

acknowledged Peterborough FC's programme notes for their home to v City in September 2001.Cardiff reach the semi-finals of the Division Two play-offs, finishing 4th in the league. Former City name Kevin Ratcliffe, now boss of Shrewsbury Town, brings his team to Ninian Park and takes away a point from a 1-1 draw. Lennie Lawrence is in charge of the Bluebirds from a 1-0 win v Bury in January.

Cup competitions: FA Cup triumph over Leeds United deflated in the next round by Tranmere Rovers. City win the Welsh Cup by 1-0 v Swansea City.

Best result: 7-1 annihilation of Rushden & Diamonds in an LDV Trophy fixture at Ninian Park highlighted by a 5 goal marksman Gavin Gordon. Oldham Athletic receives the same treatment when the Bluebirds visit in a league match.

Attendances: 22,009 see City v Leeds. United were top of the Championship when they came to Ninian Park in January. In the league, a huge 17,403 saw the City's first home game v Wycombe Wanderers. Cardiff won 1-0 with a Danny Gabbidon goal.

Cardiff finish 6th in the Nationwide League Two but win promotion through the play-offs. The Bluebirds are promoted to the top league thanks to a 1-0 win against Q.P.R at the Millennium Stadium played out in front of a mammoth 66,096 spectators. Alan Campbell nets the winner. Diminutive striking machine Robert Earnshaw surpasses Hughie Ferguson's 1926/ 1927 goal scoring record with hat tricks along the way v Tranmere Rovers and Q.P.R.
Cup competition: Spurs ko Cardiff 1-0 in a League Cup fixture away at White Hart Lane. Coventry City eliminates Cardiff from the FA Cup in a January replay.
Best result: 1-5 away victory in the League Cup in early September v Boston United.
Attendances: A good season for support with 14,702 at Ninian Park for the visit of subsequent champions Wigan in mid-April.

19,146 see the 1-0 Play-Off win v Bristol City in May.

Cardiff finish 13th in table. Robert Earnshaw scores a hat-trick v Leyton Orient in Carling Cup and a brilliant 4 goals v Gillingham in a September league win. A plethora of visits from London clubs such as West Ham, Millwall and Crystal Palace proves a highlight for the season campaign. Although Cardiff managed not a single victory against any of them!
Cup competitions: City meet Wrexham in the FAW Premier Cup which they lose on penalties after the game ended 2-2.

And so to freshly-created Coca-Cola Championship, with Cardiff playing in the newly-titled Championship, aka Division One. Ronnie Moore, a bygone City name, sees his Rotherham United side sent packing with a 2-0 defeat at Ninian Park. Past terrace favourite Nathan Blake also returns as a late substitute for Leicester in an exciting 0-0 draw.
Cup competitions: Cardiff do Wales proud, forcing Premiership side Blackburn Rovers to a replay in the F.A Cup. Lennie Lawrence put's out a reserve side for the FAW Premier Cup and sees his side beaten 1-0 by Bangor.
to be continued...

Cardiff City v Bristol City - 14/04/1945

A War Cup fixture attended by 23, 161 saw the sides take a mammoth three hours and 22 minutes to finally find a winner. Kicking off at 3pm, the sides would continue playing until 6.40pm. As full-time arrived, the score was 2-2 and an extra 20 minutes was played and on it went as the referee allowed additional time until Cardiff man Colin Gibson eventually scored over 100 minutes later. He was so exhausted that he could not get up to celebrate! Not one cramp-riddled player was allowed to be substituted in those days.

Cardiff City 1 v Bristol City 1

'Cardiff invaded for City's holiday game.' S.W. Echo, 7/04/ 7. For this Monday game against local rivals Bristol, the queue for tickets began some hours prior to the kick-off. The Echo deemed it the 'needle match of the season', memorable for a City fan falling throw the roof of the Grange End. He injured himself and four others. 51,000+ were present that day, the game was the highest attended fixture in the country and set a new attendance record for a Third Division fixture.

all things city a-z

Ivor Allchurch

With so many players having turned out for the City over the years, it would be impossible to include all the names that I should have liked but what you will find on the following pages is still pretty comprehensive.

Ivor ALLCHURCH

A 'complete footballer, giant of a captain.

The golden boy of Welsh football.' Allchurch was awarded an M.B.E for his services to sport in 1966 and seemingly not a bad word was ever said against him. Transferred to Cardiff City in 1962 for £20,000, Ivor remained at the club until 1967 announcing his retirement from the game. This graceful, wizard-like player whom, "you could do nothing but admire." [Former England manager, Ron Greenwood] made his City debut against Newcastle United. Of course, the inside-right star scored twice as well! Ivor, as with fellow City player, Trevor Ford, also played for Swansea Town.

His record is impressive: 251 goals scored, 68 full Wales caps with 24 goals scored at that level. He was the star of the Cardiff City winning side in the Welsh Cup final of 1964/5 and it was his goal that won the trophy for Swansea the next season. Whilst at the Vetch Field with the Swans, Allchurch made his debut against Cardiff on Christmas Eve 1949. Watched by 27,264 he soon became a terrace favourite and made his first Welsh international appearances whilst sill a Swans player. Coincidentally, Ivor played alongside his brother Len whilst there. Consistently hitting hat tricks and four goals in games, his obvious talent was soon capitalized upon and he was sold from Swansea to Newcastle United before City paid £18,000 for his services. In a City shirt he scored 120 goals in 35 league games. Not only that, he was the top scorer for the club in seasons 1963/64 and 1964/65. He produced a hat trick against former club Swansea in the following season and another two in the second leg final of the Welsh Cup v Wrexham. Accumulating 68 Welsh caps, he moved back to play for the Swans and netted a total of 43 times in 126 games. Ivor continued playing well on into his fifties in the lower leagues of Welsh football and it was his goal for Wales that took them to the quarter-finals of the 1958 World Cup where they were beaten 1-0 by eventual tournament winners Brazil. He died in 1997.

Adrian ALSTON

'I love running at people and attacking them on the deck.' Alston was originally seen as a midfielder rather than as a striker prior to arriving at Ninian Park in October 1975 but it is as a forward that he is remembered at City. A dream debut saw him score in a 4-3 home defeat of Chesterfield. Adrian was sold to Tampa Bay Rowdies for £23,000 in December '76 and replaced at City by the brilliant Robin Friday. He represented Australia in the 1974 World Cup Finals in Germany and played 60 times for the City scoring 24 goals.

Willie ANDERSON

Last known to be a radio executive in America Willie arrived at the Ninian Park club in 1972 after being blooded by the late Matt Busby at Manchester United alongside George Best. A move to Aston Villa followed before a spell in south Wales and departure in the summer months

of 1977. The 1975/76 promotion-winning Cardiff season proved to be his best and it was Anderson that set up many of the goals smashed in by Tony Evans and Adrian Alston. Liverpool-born, he made a total of 126 appearances for Cardiff and scored 12 times.

Aston VILLA

Thursday 1 September 1910. 7,000 see City's first professional player to be registered as such, Jack Evans, scores the first goal for the Bluebirds against the Villa that day.

Billy AYRE

Spent his considerable career as a player and manager/coach of lower league teams. Ayre was Blackpool manager in the promotion-winning 1990/91 season [and the following one] when City played against them. A true club legend at Blackpool he brought his far-reaching experience to both Cardiff and Swansea, assisting Jan Molby at the Vetch Field before coming to Ninian Park. He died 2004.

Billy BAKER

'A player of tremendous capabilities: bags of ability and the stamina to go with it.' Proclaimed Jimmy Scoular. Known as 'Puffer'

whilst at Ninian Park from 1938 to 1955 having made over 300 appearances. He first wore the number seven City shirt during the 1938/1939 season and made 30+ appearances until his last season as a Bluebird. Departed from Ninian Park for Ipswich and subsequently returned to the city working as an ambulance driver.

Colin BAKER

'I had a good run and loved every minute.' A stocky little fella, Baker was born in the Tremorfa area of Cardiff in 1934 and is remembered as one of City's greatest wing-halves. Whilst a Bluebird, Colin gained one of his 7 caps for Wales in an international v Scotland played at Ninian Park in October 1960. Wales won the game 2-0. With a debut coming in the last game of the '53/'54 season in a tie v Sheffield Wednesday. Aged nineteen, a 2-2 draw came amidst his National Service secondment. Colin retired from football at the end of the '65/'66 season after scoring a little over a half-dozen goals as a Bluebird over a 14 year period and 352 appearances notched up. The City programme notes summed up his contribution; 'One of the most loyal servants of the club.'

Gary BELL

'One of the most stylish full-backs in the Second Division.' Goal magazine. Former factory clerk Gary cost the Bluebirds a paltry £750 from a local West Midlands side in February 1966 and he progressed on to make the most league appearances in a City shirt over the course of the 1970/1971 season. Bell featured in the famous 1-0 victory over Real Madrid and was struck on the leg by a broken bottle whilst playing in the 2-0 away return fixture at the Bernabeau Stadium. His debut in the City defence came in a 7-1 defeat by Wolves at Molineux in September '66. It was one of 2 such score lines, the other being v Plymouth Argyle, which Gary also played in! Some 8 years later he left for Newport County with Jimmy Scoular.

Dave BENNETT

'If I did well last season at Main Road, I want to go one better here. I've a whole host of targets including a winner's medal at Wembley and playing for England!' Joining City from Manchester City and an FA Cup winner with Coventry City, the club he signed for after scoring nineteen times for Cardiff during his two seasons: 1981/ 1982 & 1982/1983. The latter being a promotion-gaining season whilst the former saw the Bluebirds relegated! 'Benno' played in the same Cardiff City team with his younger brother Gary. Dave scored on his home debut in 1-0 win v Barnsley after City paid £120,000 for his services. Also captured the attention by scoring on his away debut at Sheffield Wednesday, notching up 5 goals in his

first league campaign with the Bluebirds. Bennett netted 12 times in 40 appearances linking up well with another Ninian Park favourite, Jeff Hemmerman. He went on to score in the '87 FA Cup final.

Gary BENNETT

'A very adventurous player.' Former City defender and club team mate Keith Pontin. Transferred to Sunderland in summer 1984 subsequently completing some 463 games for the club who were then managed by his former City chief Len Ashurst. Manchester-born younger brother of Dave, was a lanky central defender with a penchant for goals in the promotion winning '82-'83 season in which he scored six times. Cardiff finished second to Portsmouth in what was then the old Division Three. The brothers both scored in two City matches: a 3-1 home win against Walsall and a 3-0 demolition again at home, this time v Millwall. Gary joined the Bluebirds from Manchester City in September 1981 after being convinced by Tony Brook and Ritchie Morgan. His older brother Dave followed three days later. After retiring from the playing side of football, Gary managed Darlington and is still at the club but in a training capacity nowadays.

George BEST

Bestie played in an international fixture at Ninian Park in July 1969 but not in an Ireland shirt. No, George was playing in a Rest of the UK v Wales charity raiser. At the Cottagers, he made 42 appearances and scored 8 goals over the 1976/ 1977 season and some of the early part of following. He was quoted in the local press as being very impressed with the City team that beat Fulham in the 1976-77 campaign. Bringing fans back to football to see The George Best Show with supporting players Rodney Marsh and Bobby Moore, Bestie played in the Division Two fixture at Ninian Park, a 3-1 defeat on 24 September 1977. Shortly after, the former European Footballer of the Year returned to the American Soccer League. Ex-

City captain Mike England was already there.

Doug BLAIR & Jimmy BLAIR

'Dougie' made 222 appearances in a Cardiff shirt over 7 years from 1947 onwards. The Yorkshire-born lad scored 29 goals for the club. His father, Jimmy [seen opposite] played for the Bluebirds in the 1920s and was also a City skipper and Scottish international. Following retirement he was a coach at City.

Nathan BLAKE

Blake came to professional football at Newport County and subsequently played for Cardiff City,

his hometown, from 1989 through to the 1993-94 season wherein he was transferred to Sheffield United for £300,000. Born in Cardiff back in 1972, Nathan collected 164 appearances for the Bluebirds and hit the net on 40 occasions as the club spiralled down 3 divisions. His debut for City came in an away match at Eastville, where the Bluebirds were beaten 2-1 by Bristol Rovers. He popped in a hat trick during a 1993 Ninian Park fixture v Stockport County memorable for a debut being given to Andy Legg. Blake was a decent goal scorer and a powerful header of the ball, a particular example being the brilliant goal he scored for Wales v Norway in October 2000. As a City player in the number 10 shirt Nathan hit a left foot curler into the top right corner of the Manchester City goal in a '94 FA Cup tie; he beat half the team to do this. Having just moved to Sheffield, Blake and former City team-mate Jason Perry both made

their international debuts together in a friendly v Norway at Ninian Park back in 1994. Blake joined Leicester City, from Wolves, in 2004 with ex-Bluebirds boss Alan Cork initially employed by the Foxes as assistant-manager. 'Blakey' came on to a rousing welcome [as substitute] for their visit to Ninian Park in a goal less draw in October 2004. Now at Wolves.

Bluebirds name

The Bluebird - a symbolist play written by Belgian playwright Maurice Maeterlinck. The work was being performed in Cardiff back during the period when the club was formed and may go some way in explaining its special connection to the club.

Bob Bank

"I've watched games from behind both goals, and from both sides of the pitch. I'm impressed by the Bob Bank." Football fan Laurence New. The 'Popular Bank' officially but nobody ever calls it thus and never have done. Originally costing a shilling's admission, it has been a rough place in its composition and suitably realigned later on in its life as the main throng of the City diehard. It remained uncovered until work in the summer of 1958 gave shelter to spectators for the first time. "I could often get an idea of the score by the roar of the crowd," remembers exiled City fan David Hanson, "but to be sure I would stand by my gate and ask 'what was the score mister?' to the first man coming past our house on Ninian Park road. " David and his father always stood on the Bob Bank together, "With our backs to the railway, and if anybody swore, I mean

bloody or bugger, my father would warn them to cut it out." A terrace was installed, consisting of concrete stepping and by the 2001/ 2002 season further alterations resulted in an increased capacity with standing facilities available at the front. Its right-hand corner now has match p.a. system but back on the open Bank of the 1950s a hospital broadcast box was once positioned. Over the summer months of 2001 the faded lettering on its corrugated roof was removed. The Captain Morgan's Rum signage had been there since the roof's construction in 1958 and although no advertising was painted initially, following City's promotion to Division One the Captain first made his appearance.

Paul BODIN

'Football can be a cynical game sometimes.' Cardiff-born defender and Welsh International who played for the City in the 1980s. Paul will always be remembered for that penalty for Wales v Romania at Cardiff Arms Park which hit the crossbar in a vital World Cup qualifier match. The Welsh lost the match 2-1 and failed to reach the finals in America. Despite this, he gained two additional caps for his country. A well-travelled professional, his debut came v Wrexham at Ninian Park in the opening fixture of the 1982/ 1983 season. City lost 1-2. The match was a memorable one as it gave debuts for Bodin and 4 other debutants; Jeff Hemmerman, Roger Gibbins, David Tong and Steve Humphries [in goal, and in his only appearance in a City shirt]. After leaving the club he turned out for Newport County, Crystal Palace, Swindon and Wycombe. Paul now works as a Director of Football at Swindon College.

Terry BOYLE

Another of the City captains during his career at the club which spanned 3 years from 1986 to 1989. Born in west Wales, Terry put in 167 first-team appearances mixed with a collection of 10 goals. After exiting Ninian Park Boyle established himself as the Newport County skipper. Capped 4 times for Wales, he returned to play at Cardiff as a Merthyr Tydfil player for a Welsh Cup tie in November 1990.

John BUCHANAN

'I'll tell you one thing for sure - there's no feeling quite like it when you hit one just right from long range and it smacks into the back of the net!' Signing from Northampton Town 'Buchie' marched on to clock up a mammoth 400 playing appearances in a 12-year, seven seasons stay at City. Awarded the

Cardiff City Player of the Season Award for the '78/ '79 season, he was the leading scorer with 16, John possessed a lethal shot for a midfielder. An example of his cannon ball shooting prowess was demonstrated in a 3-3 home draw with Swansea City in 1980. He came to the club back in October 1974 and scored 67 goals over 265 appearances in a Cardiff shirt.

Alan CAMPBELL

'A model professional.'
Richie Morgan, former Cardiff player and manager. Scots-born Campbell was transferred to City from Birmingham City in March '76 whilst City were a Division Two side. In total, Alan played 190 times for the club and put in a couple of goals.

Canton Stand / Spar Family Stand

With success coming for Cardiff during the immediate post war years, debts were sufficiently wiped to allow the construction of the 4,000 seater Canton stand which commenced in 1919 and was completed a year or so later. Signage for Franklyn's Tobbaco used to cover its roof and its unusual [and quite frankly *very* uncomfortable] bench-type seating in later years has since been replaced. Present chairman Sam Hamman, owner of supermarket chain Spar, replaced much of the old stand when it was reopened as the Spar Family Stand in 2002. The stand was unique in that it was the only one in the Football League of its kind; most clubs did not have seating directly behind their goals like Cardiff had.

Clive CHARLES

The first black player to take the captain mantle at City for the 1974-75 season. A brace short of a century of appearances in a City shirt, he subsequently left in the exodus of football talent off to the American Soccer League.

John CHARLES

'A giant among players.' Denis Law.
The man known as the Il Buon Gigante aka the 'gentle giant' with a physique of Charles Atlas was born in Swansea as was brother Mel, also a future City shirt-wearer. Charles made a successful career at Leeds, Juventus and Roma before being tempted back to Wales. He joined Cardiff City in August 1963 following a number of players being sold by the club to facilitate his £22,000 transfer fee from Roma. Over the course of his two and a half seasons at Ninian Park John scored 19 goals in 88 appearances. Brother Mel was playing for

The Canton stand

City upon the arrival of his younger brother and he was eventually to lose his place in the team to John. It had been as a 17 year-old at Leeds that he had played as a centre-half before being reshaped into a centre forward where he made a real name for himself. Never one to do anything ordinarily, John's full debut at Ninian Park was a curious affair. Playing Norwich City in a Division Two match on 24 August 1963 problems with his transfer fee almost preventing his arrival, which was seen by 22,078. Charles scored a freak goal just before half-time with the score at 1-1. The Bluebirds were awarded an indirect free kick, near the half-way line, when, the Gentle Giant, struck the ball and it hit the head of 'keeper Kevin Keelan and in to the net! However, author Marlo Risoli's biography states that it hit the keeper's shoulder. In 1950, aged eighteen, Charles was then the youngest player to be capped at full level by Wales. Hailed as the greatest Welsh player ever, at one stage he and Trevor Ford, another City legend, competed for the number 9 shirt. In all, Charles accumulated 38 international caps and was neither cautioned nor sent off throughout his entire career. He left City to join Hereford United as player-manager in the summer of 1966. Returning with the club to play against Cardiff in the 1968 Welsh Cup final, he even scored. For more information read King John, the man's autobiography. Born in 1931 he was awarded a C.B.E in 2001 and died in 2004.

Top right: Mel and John Charles at Cardiff City.

Mel CHARLES
The older brother to John, weighing 13st and measuring 6ft, Melfyn played for Cardiff and Swansea, the latter of which he regularly struck hat-tricks over a seven year period. Like his brother, Mel signed professional terms with Swansea Town and had the good fortune to play in the 1958 World Cup Finals in Sweden. An excellent header of the ball Mel arrived at City in 1962 from Arsenal for £27,000 where he had played at centre half and centre forward; just like John at Leeds. Subsequently losing his place in the Cardiff team to his younger brother who had returned from playing in Italy, Mel left in the summer '65 after scoring 25 goals in 79 games. He had made his Bluebirds debut in a 0-0 v Manchester City in March '62. In the red of Wales Mel scored all 4 goals in an international played at Ninian Park in April '62. In all, Mel struck more than a hundred goals. His son, Jeremy , was also capped for Wales and played for Swansea.
Ken CHISHOLM
'A clever inside-forward with a

strong shot.' The Glasgow-born 'Chis' made his Cardiff City debut during the 1951/ 1952 season after switching to the Bluebirds in March '52 from Coventry. He went on to nab 10 goals in the remaining matches. By the following season he made the number 10 shirt his own with 13 goals netted for the Bluebirds. He left City in the midst of the 1953/ 1954 Division One campaign that saw the side finish in 10th position.Ken's goal tally worked out at 33 in 66 appearances in a blue shirt. A full Scottish international, he passed away in 1990.

City KIT

"Shirts royal blue, white collars and sleeves, knickers: white. Stockings: royal blue, white tops." 1952 programme description of city colours! As Riverside, the club wore a kit consisting of chocolate and amber quartered shirts with black shorts (or 'knickers' as they called them back then). However, when Cardiff City played their first friendly at Ninian Park v Aston Villa there kit had changed to blue shirts, white shorts and blue socks.

Brian CLARK

'He's got such a placid personality.' Don Clark, Brian's father and a former Bristol City striker. Enjoyed two spells at Ninian Park in a playing career spanning eighteen years from 1960 - 1978. It was Clark, in the blue number 9 shirt, who scored a famous header against Real Madrid for City in the European Cup Winners' Cup. He was a formidable goal-scorer and was top scorer for the Bluebirds in seasons 1969/70, 1970/71 and 1971/72, in which campaign he notched up his 150th goal. His full debut came for Cardiff away at Derby County and he scored on his home debut in a 2-0 defeat of Preston. As a striking partner for big John Toshack, Clarke won 4 Welsh Cup winners medals. He left the club in 1972 but returned during the '75-'76 season which saw City promoted from Division Three. In total Brian scored 108 goals [more than 200 in all his career] for the Bluebirds and ended his playing days at Newport County, where he continued to knock them in. He became the Ironsides reserve coach whilst at Somerton Park.After retiring, he managed Maesteg AFC.

Brian CLOUGH

A terrier-like footballer and full England inter-national whose playing career was overlooked by his managerial maestro. "Old Big 'ead" gained his first cap, aged 24, in a 1959 interna-tional v Wales at Ninian Park. The game was drawn 1-1 and it was to be the penultimate cap for the future boss at this level. Cloughie returned to Cardiff's ground as manager of Derby County in 1967 and of Nottingham Forest in the 1976/ 1977 season push that saw his side take away a 3-0 victory. Danny Malloy, a City central defender had a bit of an clash with a younger Brian Clough during a Cardiff v Middlesborough game which resulted in the latter being laid out on the pitch! The referee on that September 1958 day failed to see the incident. A further face off occurred in the Ninian Park tunnel following Mr Clough's assessment of City seeing him being throttled by the then Bluebirds manager. Strangely enough neither incident was recorded in his autobiography.

Club Address

Ninian Park, Sloper Road, Cardiff Cf11 8SX.

Club HONOURS

FA Cup Winners 1927

FA Cup Finalists 1925

FA Charity Shield Winners 1927

Welsh Cup Winners 1912, 1920, 1922, 1923, 1927, 1928, 1930, 1956, 1959, 1964, 1965, 1967, 1968, 1969, 1970, 1971, 1973, 1974, 1976, 1988, 1992, 1993

Wartime League West Cup Winners 1944/1945

FAW Premier Cup Winners 2002

Division Four Runners Up 1988

Division Three Champions [S] 1947

Division Three Champions 1993

Division Three Runners-Up 1976, 1983, 2001

Division Three Third Place 1999

Division Two Runners-Up 1921, 1952, 1960

Division Two Play-Off Winners 2003

Division One Runners-Up 1924

European Cup Winners' Cup Semi-Finalists 1968

Alan CURTIS

'So strong and so skilful.'

Ex-City team mate Jason Perry.

A player and later coach forever linked with Swansea City, nonetheless Curtis enjoyed two spells as a Cardiff City player. Brought to Ninian Park by Frank Burrows, Alan was selected 35 times for Wales and arrived on a free transfer in 1986 making his debut at home in a drab 0-0 draw v Rochdale. He played 157

times for the Bluebirds and was a big influence in the club's promotion surge in the '87/'88 campaign. They also won the Welsh Cup that year too with Alan scoring in a 2-0 victory v Wrexham. May 1988 marked his 500th appearance as a professional with Crewe providing opposition. Alan remained until 1989 when he returned to Swansea City. He scored 13 goals for the City and a total of 115 for the 5 different clubs he served. Following a massive 570 appearances in his playing career, Alan retired in 1991. Now a part of the John Toshack-centred national side.

Ernie CURTIS

Cardiff-born and a full Wales international Ernie made 70 appearances and scored 15 goals for the club during his career. He turned pro in 1926 and went on to play in the FA Cup winning side of the following season when, aged 19, he was the youngest player to do so. Ernie joined Birmingham after Cardiff but returned in 1933. After the 1939-45 war Curtis became a trainer at Ninian Park [picured above whilst working in a coaching role].

Carl DALE

'Fit, fast and very mobile.'

Jason Perry, former City player.

Whilst a Bluebird from 1991 to 1997 he played in every game of the '91/'92 season bar the first home match against Lincoln City. Arriving at Ninian Park from Chester City for a fee of £100,000, Colwyn Bay-born Carl struck the winning goal in the Welsh Cup final against Hednesford Town played at the National Stadium and seen by 11,000 fans. He scored his first goal for the Bluebirds on his debut in an away 1-1 draw at Crewe Alexandra. Although hampered by injuries he helped City to promotion in the 1992/ 1993 season by netting 11 times. Overall, he made 276 appearances over 7 seasons and struck 108 goals. Born in 1966 Carl left Ninian Park for Yeovil Town but would return with Town for an FA Cup tie v Cardiff in 1999. The Bluebirds gave him a testimonial match at City in May '99.

Len DAVIES

Scoring a total of 148 goals for the City Mr Davies played 338 games for the Bluebirds during the course of a ten year/ 12 seasons career. Len's debut came in a defeat in September 1921 and made his final appearance against Spurs in April 1931, watched by 6,666. That season the Bluebirds were relegated. He netted the first hat trick by a City player in a game at Ninian Park against Bradford City [he also hit 4 goals in an away game v W.B.A.]. In his first season at the club, City reached the semi-finals of the FA Cup and won the Welsh Cup. It was Davies, the 23 goals in a season man, that missed the penalty against Birmingham in the 1921/ 1922 season. What's unusual about that? Well, it was this miss that meant City lost the Division One Championship purely by goal average! Len hit the ball straight at the keeper's feet. The Splott-born striker died of pneumonia in 1945.

Fred DAVIS

'Strong, agile and dependable...'
Cardiff was the second club for this goalkeeper who hailed from Liverpool and had originally made a name at Wolves. As the number one at City, he played in 128 matches with his debut arriving via a 3-0 win v Portsmouth in 1968. He left in 1970.

Mark DELANEY

Scored a solitary goal for the Bluebirds before moving on to the Premiership with Aston Villa in 1999 for a transfer fee of £600,000. But what a goal it was: he ran from the half-way line as the ball was played in front of him and holding off a strong challenge from a Chester City defender, he slotted the ball into the right-hand corner of the keeper's net. It was a November 1988 match that Cardiff won handsomely 6-0. Presently a regular for Wales.

Andy DIBBLE

Still playing competitive football in the 2004/ 05 season, Andy gained the first of his three Welsh cap as a goal keeper back in 1986. He was brought on at Ninian Park as a sixteen-year-old at the time when Bob Hatton, a part-time Insurance broker and 36-year-old striker also arrived. Dib's full debut at home being in a 1-0 defeat by Crystal Palace in May 1982. It was in the course of the '82/ '83 season that Andy played a lot of games with 17 of his 20 appearances seeing City unbeaten. By the succeeding season he would miss only one game as the City stopper. As is always the case, his consistency was soon noticed by clubs in the higher leagues and he was sold to Luton Town. As their 'keeper he helped the club win the Littlewoods Cup in 1989. A plethora of clubs have since enjoyed his services ranging from Rangers to a box full of non-league sides.

Phil DWYER

'First and foremost, the man is simply one of the great competitors.' Manager Jimmy Scoular, 1978.One of few names for the mantle of most loved City player. Phil played 10 times for Wales and for City he was a defender, midfield and striker with equal ability success. 'Joe' as he was nicknamed, due to a physical resemblance to Joe Royle, turned pro with the Bluebirds aged 18. He made his debut at Ninian Park against Orient, watched by 6,000. His final appearance came in a 1-4 defeat at home to Notts County on 17 February 1985. Playing for Wales at his club ground in 1977, Phil scored a header v England and Peter Shilton. Despite breaking his leg after a wardrobe fell on it he went on to wear a City shirt 573 times and score a half-century of goals. [Pictured above and with Alan Curtis]

Robert EARNSHAW

'He has that goalscoring knack. It's something you can't teach.' John Toshack, Wales manager, 2004.Born in Zambia but growing up in Caerphilly, Cardiff, 'Earnie' made quite a name for himself as a scorer blessed with blistering pace. He made his full professional debut for Cardiff City v Hartlepool in August 1998 after turning professional. He managed to grab a goal in that 1-1 draw. After making his way through the ranks as a YTS youngster in 1997,

Earnshaw initially played for the first team in a fixture v Wrexham back in October 1997. With his league debut arriving courtesy of a scoreless draw with Brighton in 1998. above: Consistency in his goal scoring came during the 2000/ 2001 season with 'Earnie' becoming a firm favourite at Ninian Park as the club's top scorer. As a Bluebird he struck 7 hat-tricks amongst a total of 107 first class goals for the side. His scoring celebrations were presented in the form of summersaults and are fondly remembered by those that saw them! Now an established Welsh international, he left Cardiff City amidst much consternation amongst City fans for premiership strugglers West Bromwich Albion in 2004 for close to £4 million.

Jeff ECKHARDT

Born in the steel city of Sheffield, Jeff [seen opposite]made his debut for Cardiff against Brighton in August 1996 after a transfer from Stockport County in August 1996. The goals and appearances then flowed. Jeff was most recently playing for Welsh side Merthyr Tydfil.

Mike ENGLAND

Made his name whilst a Tottenham player with the White Hart Lane club breaking a British transfer fee record of £95,000 back in 1962. Talked out of retirement by Jimmy Andrews, Mike was City captain during the 1975/ 76 season making 40 appearances. His debut came in a 1-2 cup defeat at the hands of Bristol Rovers. As a centre-half he collected 38 Wales caps: 28 of them as captain and made his international debut v N.Ireland at Ninian Park in 1962. He was tempted back from the USA, and subsequently returned there to play in the North American Soccer League afterwards. A backroom job or even management roles at City was said to have been on the agenda following the end of a promotion-winning season. Mike played for Team America against England in 1976. He was selected for Wales in what resulted in a 1-1 draw v Hungary at Ninian Park in March 1963. He eventually managed the Welsh national team for four years from 1980 [starting with a 2-1 defeat by Austria.] Ex-City star Doug Livermore was his Number Two over this period which saw the national side re-ignited in its purpose. Mike was awarded the MBE in 1984.

European Cup Winners' CUP

Inception in the 1960/ 1961 season.
Cardiff are pitched in their first match of the competition away to Norwegian side Esbjerg in September 1964. They draw 0-0 and win the return leg 1-0 at Ninian Park. City march on to the Quarter finals after defeating holders Sporting Lisbon before a crowd of 38,458 they go out 2-3 on aggregate to Real Zaragoza. 'The Welsh side fought bravely in a match that was over-robust and provided many free-kicks.' Real were the present holders of the Inter-Cities Fairs Cup at the time and doing well in the Spanish First Division.

1967/ 1968 season
'I have always thought that we should have beaten SV Hamburg...but they beat us in the 2nd leg at Ninian Park when we were really the better side. We were so near yet so far from European glory that evening!' Jimmy Scoular. A fantastic campaign from the Bluebirds sees them reach the semi-finals.
Quarter-finals v Moscow Torpedo 1-0 at Ninian Park.'Cardiff do Wales proud.'
8,000 mile round trip for away leg in March '68 played in Tashkent, 2,000 miles away from Moscow which was experiencing sub-zero temperatures. City lose 1-0. A third match to decide who goes through is arranged in Germany which City win 1-0. Future City manager Richie Morgan makes his debut for the club in place of an injured Don Murray.
'A magnificent feat of spirit and determination.'
Semi-finals v Hamburg 1-1 away, 2-3 at home.
1968/ 1969 season v FC Porto 2-2 home, 2-1 away. City beat German side Werder Bremen over two legs.
1969/ 1970 season
Cardiff take care of Norwegian side Mjoendalen I.F. by 12-2 on aggregate but are knocked-out

by Turkish champions Goeztepe Izmir 3-1 over the two legs. Reserve striker Sandy Allan collects a hat trick in the former.

1970/ 1971 season
Cardiff beat debutants PO Larnaca and FC Nantes on the way to a quarter-final meeting with the sleek Real Madrid.

"It was a crowd of over 60,000," recollects Di Rowland, " and waiting outside to get in there was not one ounce of space. A man had a cigarette and he could not stub it out as the crowd was so dense. " Incredibly, City won 1-0 at Ninian Park and their same 11 played in the return leg which Madrid took 2-0. Teen-aged Nigel Rees hit the cross for the famous Brian Clark header at Ninian Park. Real made it to the final where they were beaten 2-1 in a replay by Chelsea.

1971/ 1972 season v Dynamo Berlin. First round leg in September '71 in an evening kick-off at Ninian Park results in a 1-1 draw. A programme for that night's game cost 5p. By season 2004-05 it would be up to £2.50. For the away leg, the winners had to arrive via a penalty shoot-out. Cardiff lost 4-5.

1973/ 1974 season v Sporting Lisbon 0-0 at Ninian Park.

1974/ 1975 season v Ferencvaros. City beaten 2-0 away and 1-4 at Ninian Park in October.

1976/ 1977 season
City eliminate Swiss side Servette on the away goals rule in the preliminary round and meet Dynamo Tiblisi in the 1st round proper. They take a light 1-0 lead to the return leg but are beaten 3-0.

1977/ 1978 season
Despite losing in the Welsh cup Final to Shrewsbury Town City qualify for the ECWC once again. Just over 3.5k see the goal-less 1st round tie v FK Austria Memphis at Ninian Park. The return leg sees a 1-0 defeat for City.

1988/ 1989 season
Following a break of more than a decade Cardiff play again in the ECWC.
Irish side Derry City are soundly quashed but City are beaten 1-2 at Ninian Park and 4-0 away to Danish team Aarhus.

1992/ 1993 season v Admira Wacker 1-1 at Ninian Park & 0-2 away.

1993/ 1994 season v Standard Liege 5-2 away & 1-3 at home. City had played the Belgian side back in 1965 and had lost both ties. For a concise overview of all the Welsh clubs fortunes in European football you could do no better than get a copy of Red Dragons in Europe: A Complete Record. See bibliography.

Jack EVANS
'The Bala Bang.'
The first Cardiff City footballer to be officially registered as such by the fledgling club. Jack possessed a good, strong shot and was also the first Cardiff player to become a full Welsh international, capped as he was, 8 times.
A Welsh speaker and ex-Wrexham man, Jack received a signing on fee from City of 6 shillings and was paid 35/- a week. It was Evans who scored the first goal for Cardiff City at Ninian Park, in a friendly with Aston Villa in 1910. He played an astonishing 395 times for the Bluebirds prior to a move to Bristol Rovers.

Tony EVANS

'He's some player, quick and skilful.' Robin Friday, team mate. Hailing from Liverpool, Tony came to Ninian Park on a free transfer from Blackpool during the summer of 1975 ready for the oncoming '75/ '76 season. He scored 31 times in 57 appearances as a Cardiff City player and was top scorer in the promotion-gaining team of 1976. He was again the leading hitman for the Bluebirds in the '77/ '78 campaign and netted all four in a League Cup match away to Bristol Rovers. Evans worked really well in a forward line for Cardiff that included Doug Livermore and Adrian Alston as well as alongside his opposite number Robin Friday. The City penalty-taker saw a niggling thigh injury restrict his role in the '77/ '78 season and he left Ninian Park for Birmingham City at the end of that period. By the beginning of the next campaign he made a swift return in a Brum shirt at Ninian Park. 'Small, sharp and a perfect foil for the big centre forward.' Summarized City boss Jimmy Andrews. Tony's full playing career record is admirable, 62 goals in 153 appearances in the blue shirt of Cardiff City.

The FA Cup

The League Cup may have returned in the commercial guise of the Milk Cup, Littlewoods Cup or whatever else Cup but the FA Cup largely remains untarnished by an external sponsor. In 1927, Cardiff City were the only

non-English club to win the trophy in all of its long and regal history. In a team made up of 3 Welsh men, 3 Scots, 4 Irish and 1 English, City took the trophy out of England following a 1-0 victory against the mighty Arsenal. The Bluebirds reached the final in 1925 as well as the semis in 1921, and the last eight in both 1922 and 1924. Since those heady days, the City have never made it to another final but still there record in the cup is a decent one: 218 matches played [up until 2004] with 88 victories, 52 draws and 78 defeats. One of the most stunning FA Cup wins came in a Sunday tea-time win v Leeds United in January 2002 with a 2-1 win recorded by the Bluebirds. The match was screened live on Sky.

famous players to play /score at ninian.

Peter SHILTON

Filled the keeper role for Leicester City at Ninian Park back in '69, 'Shilts' returned in a 1980s cup tie as Southampton keeper. Teased by the crowd that evening after his alleged marital indiscretions had fortuitously been splashed across newspapers he gave the crowd the finger! I remember this as I was sitting on the uncomfortable wooden seating of the old Grange end. First played professionally as a 16 year old, he was again in goal for Leicester in the 1970/ 1971 season league match here.

Rodney MARSH
Played against Cardiff in away fixtures across the 1969 and 1971/ 1972 seasons as a Q.P.R team member. Marsh was a Fulham player in the 1976/ 77 season but didn't feature in the league fixture against City due to injury. The Cottagers were his last club player he featured in a 1961 game v Wales and in 2 others.

John GORMAN
Former Spurs player also in the Carlisle United team with Bob Hatton for their visit to Ninian Park in the 1970/ 1971 season that saw them beaten 4-0.

Ron ATKINSON
[pictured opposite]Better known for his hot and cold management career and foot-in-mouth commentary skills 'Big Ron' played for Oxford on numerous occasions in the mid-60s. He turned out for the visitors in a 1-0 defeat at Ninian Park in 1971.

Phil PARKES
Transferred to Queens Park Rangers in 1970 this future West Ham legend kept goal for the visitors in a 1-0 defeat by Cardiff at Ninian Park in the 1970/ 1971 season[opposite].

Bryan 'Pop' ROBSON
Was in the West Ham side along with Trevor Brooking and Billy Bonds that played in a 2-1 away win at Cardiff during the 1971/ 1972 season.

Trevor BROOKING

Now high up in the English F.A Brooking made his football baptism in the claret shirt of West Ham United in 1967. Awarded an M.B.E in 1981, he scored the winning goal for the Hammers in the 1980 FA Cup Final. Turned out for the East End club in a league tie at Ninian Park back in the 1971/ 1972 season.

Tommy DOCHERTY
Better known as a manger, 'The Doc' played alongside Denis Law for Scotland v Wales at Cardiff in 1958. That game was one of the 15 full caps that he collected as a player prior to moving in to management at Chelsea. Docherty was Rotherham boss in 1967 for their visit to Cardiff which resulted in a 2-2 draw. He would return to Ninian Park during the 1979/80 season as manager of a QPR team beaten 1-0. Also Man Utd, Scotland and Derby County boss.

Laurie CUNNIGHAM
West Brom and England star striker tragically killed whilst resident in Spain, Laurie had played for Orient, his first club, at Ninian Park in '77.

Dave CLEMENT
A trusty defender at Q.P.R alongside the likes of Terry Venables, Gerry Francis and Rodney Marsh in a 1971/ 1972 season visit. Collected 5 England caps as right-back, 2 of which were against Wales [both wins].

John 'Budgie' BURRIDGE
One of the games true characters 'Budgie' played for the final time between the sticks for

Scarborough in 1995, aged 46. A fitness fanatic and great keeper with a multitude of clubs collected over a lengthy career spanning 25 years. John was Blackpool keeper in their 4-3 win v City at Ninian Park in the 1971/ 1972 season. He turned pro in 1970 and serviced [amongst many others] QPR, Villa and Southampton.

Jim MONTGOMERY

Sunderland legendary keeper played in their 2-1 win 1971/ 1972 season.

Dennis TUEART

Turned out for his first club Sunderland in a 1-0 defeat during the 1971/ 1972 season campaign. Moved on to Manchester City where he really made his name.

Terry COOPER

Leeds player in the glorious side of Charlton/ Lorimar/ Bremner et al and also a Bristol City and Rovers player/manager later. Terry played v City in a Leeds 2-0 win in February 1972.

Eddie GRAY

Another Leeds player and later coach, humbled by Cardiff City in that 2002 FA Cup match.

Norman HUNTER

Plays for Leeds twice in the 1963/ 1964 season in a team that had John Charles in its firing line-up. 14,000 saw an FA Cup match that Leeds won 1-0. Hunter returned as Barnsley manager in the 1980s.

Allan CLARKE

A true goal poacher in his days as a Leeds forward of the early-1970s, Clarke scored an FA Cup Final winning goal. Moving in to management, Allan had a spell with Barnsley prior to being appointed Lincoln boss for a 1990/91 game v City. As a Leeds man, he played at Cardiff alongside Hunter, Billy Bremner and Peter Lorimar.

Jack CHARLTON

A one man club with the marvellous Leeds United side of the late 1960s-early 1970s. Jack went on to attain success as Eire manager.

Don GIVENS

Made his name as a QPR player but played as a Luton Town member in a 1-1 draw of April '72.

Bobby ROBSON

Mainly thought of as a former England manager and OAP manager of Newcastle United up until 2004, it was whilst a Fulham player that Bobby played for England in an international v Wales staged at City's ground in October 1961. Robson steered Ipswich town to FA Cup and UEFA Cup wins in 1978 and '80 respectively being replaced by former Bluebird Bobby Ferguson.

Bobby MOORE

As a West Ham player in the '65/ '66 season he was in the side that beat City away 5-3 in a League Cup tie. Moore had a torrid match in 1976 when a certain Robin Friday gave him the run-a-round. It was nearing the end of the former England captain's career though! Bobby had played for England in a 1-1 international v Wales at Cardiff in October 1961. He also played club football at Ninian in August '74, December '74, November '76 and January '77.

In total, Bobby Moore was capped 108 times for his country and played more than a thousand games until retiring in May '77.

Pat JENNINGS

A legendary keeper for both Arsenal and former club Spurs. Pat played for the Gunners at here in a 1979/1980 campaign game v City and in a pre-season friendly there in 1973 for Spurs. Kept goal for the Rest of the UK side v Wales back in 1969.

Willie YOUNG

WILLIE YOUNG ARSENAL

Played for Arsenal at Cardiff in a 1979/ 1980 fixture. Always sticks in my mind for that terrible foul on West Ham's Paul Allan in the FA CUP final of 1980.

RON SAUNDERS

Later manager of a very successful Aston Villa side, played for Portsmouth in their 2-1 away win the 1963/ 1964 season.

Arfon GRIFFITHS

Great Wrexham name as a player and manager. Griffiths played for Wrexham at City many times.

ARFON GRIFFITHS WREXHAM

Tony BOOK

Came briefly to City in the 1980s as a coach. Book had been on the opposing side at Ninian in the 1966/ 1967 season v City in an FA Cup 4th round tie.

Bobby GOULD

As a future Wales boss, Bobby was quite the goal scorer in his playing days. He   was in the Arsenal side that visited during the '68/ '69 season and left with a point in a 0-0. Bobby also helped out at Ninian Park prior to Alan Cork taking over as manager.

Eric GATES

Made his home in the thriving Ipswich Town side of the late-70s/ early 1980s alongside City boss Russell Osman. Played at Cardiff whilst with his final club Carlisle in the 1990/ 1991 season. Eric is seen opposite.

John ROBERTSON

Derby player v City in the 1983/84 season. Robertson's career highlight was as a Nottingham Forest and Scottish international.

Sam ALLARDYCE

Present Bolton manager 'Big Sam' played for Millwall at City in Jan 1983 and returned as manager of Notts Co. in the '99/ '00 season.

Gary MEGSON

A recent boss of West Brom, Megson took Robert Earnshaw to the Hawthorns early on in the 2004/ 20045 season. Played for Sheffield Wednesday at Ninian back in 1983.

Joe CORRIGAN

Recently goalkeeping-coach at Liverpool, Joe completed more than 500 appearances for Man City and was the Brighton keeper in a 2-2 draw in the 1983/ 1884 season.

1

2

3

4

5

6

Mickey THOMAS 1

Welsh international with more clubs collected as a player than most. Thomas featured in an exciting 3-3 at Ninian Park in March '84. A great little dynamo of a player.

Joey JONES

Welsh international defender and Liverpool/ Wrexham stalwart turned out for Wrexham in an exciting 3-3 draw in March '84. Also turned out for the side v City in August '82.

Peter LORIMER 2

Returned to play for Leeds United against Cardiff City in the 1983/ 1984 season. It was his second spell with the club since being a part of Don Revie's masterly side a decade earlier.

Peter BARNES

A much-travelled pro with clubs Leeds, Manchester City and West Brom. It was whilst a Leeds man that he played against City here in Wales.

Kevin KEEGAN 3

At the end of his career as player in the 1983/ 1984 season with Newcastle United the ex-Liverpool striking partner of John Toshack came to Cardiff for a league fixture.
Subsequent management roles followed with the Magpies, England, Fulham and Man City.

Terry McDERMOTT 4

'Mac' played alongside his former Liverpool team-mate Keegan in the Newcastle side of 1983/ 1984 that beat City in an away visit. Once both of their playing days were over the two joined up once again at Newcastle as manager and assistant manager.

Colin PASCOE

Works at City now as a coach. Colin played for Swansea a number of years back and as a Bluebird v the Swans in the '83/ '84 campaign.

Terry BUTCHER 5

In the same Ipswich Town side as future City manager Russell Osman that played at Ninian Park in an FA Cup match in the 1983/ 1984 season.

Mick CHANNON 6

Now a horse breeder/ trainer, Channon played for Norwich in a Milk Cup game in October '83. The Canaries were his fifth club in a playing career that totalled more than 300 goals. Bet you remember his trademark 'windmill' arm celebration upon scoring.

Mark HATELY [1 opposite page]

In the Portsmouth side that came to Cardiff in the 1983/ 1984 season. Hately spent a season with Pompey before a £1m move to AC Milan. At the tail end of his playing days Mark was appointed player-manager of Hull City and

brought his new side to Wales back in 1997.

Clive ALLEN

Played for Q.P.R in an August '79 league fixture less than a year after making his full debut. Allen left at the end of that season in another of those early £1m transfers [this time to Arsenal].

Emlyn HUGHES 2

Appointed player/manager of Rotherham in September 1981 this former Liverpool captain played for them v City whilst winding down his career. He also went on to turn out a few times for Swansea City. Sadly, 'Crazy Horse' passed away in November 2004.

Billy BREMNER 3

Forever remembered in a life-size bust outside Leeds' Elland road ground, a team that he served so well. Bremner played v Wales for a Rest of the UK side in 1969. He returned as Doncaster boss in the 1990/ 1991 season visit.

Alan HANSEN 4

Now a telly pundit alongside Gary Lineker and Mark Lawrenson, the dour Scot played for his national side in a 3-0 defeat by Wales in 1978. "Tosh scored 3." recounts Swans fan Laurence New who was there, "He wrecked Hansen. "

Brian LITTLE 5

Attained stunning league and European success as a player with Aston Villa, his only club, prior

to being the Darlington manger that visited in the 1990/ 1991 season. That season Little lead the club to the Division Four championship. Now in charge of Tranmere.

Mark LAWRENSON 6

Played v City during the mid-1970s and had a major run-in with Robin Friday at Brighton's Goldstone ground. Returned as manager of Peterborough United for their 1990/ 1991 season away fixture at Cardiff.

Gordon LEE 7

Returned with Preston to Ninian Park in the early 1980s after managing an Everton side to a successful FA Cup victory over Cardiff in the 1976/ 1977 season.

Everton Cardiff City		
(All Yellow)		(Blue with Yellow, White stripe
David LAWSON	1	Ron HEALEY
David JONES	2	Phil DWYER
Mike PEJIC	3	Brian ATTLEY
Mick LYONS	4	John BUCHANAN
Ken McNAUGHT	5	Paul WENT
Bruce RIOCH	6	Albert LARMOUR
Bryan HAMILTON	7	Steve GRAPES
Martin DOBSON	8	Doug LIVERMORE
Bob LATCHFORD	9	Tony EVANS
Duncan McKENZIE	10	Peter SAYER
Ron GOODLASS	11	David GILES

Frank WORTHINGTON

Turned out in the same Brighton side as Jimmy Case and Graham Moseley of the mid-1980s at Ninian Park.

Jimmy CASE

A past Kop idol played for Brighton v City during the 1984/ 1985 season. Still playing by the 1999/ 2000 crusade, Jimmy was on the team sheet for AFC Bournemouth's visit to Cardiff for an Autoglass Trophy tie.

Justin FASHANU

Notts County player in 1984 in an away fixture visit. The former Nottingham Forest and Norwich City man finished on the winning side in a 4-1 win.

Alan BALL

Played against Cardiff in an away fixture in 1978 with Southampton, losing 1-0. Bally returned as Portsmouth manager a few seasons later. Alan scored from a penalty in a Wales v England match in 1967.

Stan BOWLES

Scored for Q.P.R and played for Carlisle United in the 1971/ 1972 season at Cardiff when they were beaten 3-1.

Peter WITHE & Tony WOODCOCK

Both in the Clough/ Taylor Forest side which won 3-0 at Ninian in November '76.

Bob LATCHFORD

Scored for Everton in their 2-1 FA Cup win in a 1976/ 77 season tie at Ninian Park watched by 35,000. Bob also played for Swansea later on. Alongside Trevor Francis, he and Latchford were the front line in a

Birmingham City team back in the early-70s. Seen opposite.

Martin PETERS M.B.E.

Struck two times in a league cup match in the 1965/ 1966 season when his club West Ham were a Division One side and Cardiff of Second Division status. Peters made his debut for the Hammers v City on Good Friday 1962 which the visitors won 4-1. Also got a goal for England in their 3-0 win in 1967. Pictured above right.

Denis LAW

Scored for Scotland in an October 1958 international v Wales.

Jimmy GREAVES

'Greavesy' scored 44 goals in 57 appearances in an England shirt in a playing career that included Spurs, Chelsea, AC Milan and West Ham. He got his name on the score-sheet for the Three Lions during an international v Wales played at Ninian Park in October 1963. Enjoyed a second career as an ITV football pundit alongside former Liverpool and Scotland player Ian St.John in the 1980s.

Bobby CHARLTON

He of the cannonball shot honed to perfection as a youngster prior to utilizing it for both Manchester United and England. Selected for England v Wales for October 1963 and 1967 fixtures played at Ninian Park.

Martin CHIVERS

A Southampton player and goal scorer against Cardiff in their away fixture from the 1963/ 1964 season. Scores twice in a 4-2 win for Soton and another in the following season. Also as a Saint, he scored a hat trick in a 5-3 win, again played at Ninian Park, but this time in the 1965/ 1966 season. Chivers continued to be a nuisance for the Bluebirds when playing for his later club Servette Geneva in a European Cup Winners Cup tie in the 1970s.

Howard KENDALL

Scored for Preston North End in a 3-3 draw seen by 16,000 early on in the 1964/ 1965 season. Later to both play for, and manage Everton. He is pictured opposite.

Terry VENABLES

As with Bobby Robson, coincidentally also a past England manager, Venables is thought of mainly as a manager rather than for his playing career. However, as a Q.P.R competitor he scored via the penalty spot in a 4-2 away defeat against Cardiff in September 1969.

Geoff HURST

Hit two goals for West Ham in a 1965/ 1966 season match which saw the Hammers ran out as 5-3 winners. Geoff was a winning marksman for both club and country, scoring 24 goals in 49 appearances for England [hitting a brace against Wales]. He scored again in a 2-1 West Ham United win v City in the 1971/72 season.

Francis LEE

'He's so busy, always heading for goal.' John Toshack. Remembered for his days with Manchester City and Derby County, Frannie was in the Bolton side that played City in the1965/ 1966 season. He went on to score for the club at Cardiff in their 5-2 win v City in the next season. Lee hit the winning goal in a Rest of the UK v Wales match in 1969.

Trevor FRANCIS

Still a teenager when he played for Birmingham City at Ninian Park in the 1970/ 1971, '71/ '72 and '76/ '77 seasons. He scored twice in a 4-1 friendly win at Ninian Park in July 1976 before a £1.5m move took him to Nottingham Forest in 1979. Inconsistent success in a future managerial career.

Kevin HECTOR

An ace Derby County player who hit a hat trick v City in the 1967/ 68 season. Hector, seen opposite, had Alan Durban, a future Cardiff manager, in the same side for that game.

Colin ADDISON

Scored in the 4-1 defeat for Sheffield United in the 1968/ 1969 season. Addison was to be a future Barry Town/ Swansea/ Newport County [twice] and Merthyr Tydfil manager. It was whilst in charge of Hereford in the 1990/ 1991

season that he brought his side to Cardiff. City's present goalkeeping coach George Wood kept goal for the visitors then. Colin is shown opposite as Derby County manager.

Trevor CHERRY

Made his name whilst a Leeds United player but it was as captain of Huddersfield Town that Cherry scored in consecutive away fixtures here in both the 1968/1969 and 1969/1970 [championship-winning] seasons. Alongside the short-lived City boss Terry Yorath, the two ex-pros managed Bradford City in the early-1980s.

Gerry GOW

Bristol City man in their side when they made it to Division One in the late-70s. Gow played in a 1-0

win in April '71. And again in a 3-2 win for Bristol in April '72. Gerry continued to menace the Bluebirds by netting the winner for the red visitors in a July '75 league game when both clubs were in Division Three. He played for a number of teams and appeared alongside former Bluebird Ronnie Moore in a 1-2 win for Rotherham in the 1981/1982 season.

Duncan MACKENZIE

A speedy player whose prowess was ably proven in a 1976 FA Cup defeat for the Bluebirds. Mac latched on to a mistake by a City player on the half way line and ran towards the goal and scored! City were knocked out of the tournament by a 2-1 score line.

Tom FARQUHARSON

'The name...is written indelibly in the club record books.' Known in his playing days as 'Farkie' this agile, multi-talented Irishman made his mark in Gaelic football and Welsh rugby union prior to

being invited to join City. Mr T made his debut for the Bluebirds on 6 May 1922 in a 1-3 home debut v Manchester United. With his propensity for wearing a nice polo-neck sweater, he defended the Bluebirds sticks in the 1925 and crowing 1927 FA Cup finals. Retirement came for Tom after 440+ appearances a record only superseded by Phil Dwyer. He was the last link from the great 1927 team upon bowing out for City on 4 May 1935 away at Bristol City. They lost 4-0. Quite a character as a 'keeper, Tom would try to intimidate opposing players especially penalty takers, decades before Bruce Grobolaar did. He was capped at international level for both Northern Ireland and Eire. After leaving the game, he ran a tobacconist store near to the old Capitol theatre on Queen street. Tom died in Canada in 1970.

Hughie FERGUSON

'He had a phenomenal shot and with unerring accuracy he would shoot the ball

venomously into the net - usually from outside the area.'A superb goal scorer for both City and every other club, Hughie joined the Bluebirds in 1925 for £5,000 from Motherwell. It was his goal that brought the FA Cup to

Cardiff following the 1-0 victory against Arsenal. He went on to score 86 times in 130 appearances. Tragically, the gifted Ferguson took his own life after the goals dried up upon returning to play in Scotland. He was 32.

Brian FLYNN

'A nice, nippy little player.'
Scottish international Don Mason.

A tenacious battler with a successful playing and managerial career at Wrexham. Brian made his name, like Leighton James, as a professional at Burnley. Born in Port Talbot, he played for Cardiff over the 1984/ 1985 and 1985/ 1986 seasons. His time with the Bluebirds was capped by 2 consecutive relegations for the club! Brian had dominated the Leeds midfield in the years before and as a Bluebird he made 35 appearances and scored on four occasions. As a Burnley player Flynn was in the side that beat Cardiff 1-0 back in 1977. He made his City debut v Oldham in a 2-2 draw at Ninian Park watched by 3,429 in October 1984. A couple of goals were scored by Mr Flynn in a Milk Cup 1st leg tie against Swansea City at Ninian Park. By November 1985 the Welsh international had left the club. Establishing a great FA Cup giant-killing tradition as Wrexham manager in the 1990s, Flynn also had a stint as Swansea City boss in later years. A number of return visits as Wrexham boss, a job he held for nearly 12 years up until August 2001, occurred with mixed success. December 2004 saw him appointed by manager John Toshack as supervisor of the under 17 - 21 national sides.

Mike FORD

Turned pro aged eighteen and played as a full back, central defender and midfielder for the Bluebirds. As a part of the 1987/ 88 promotion-winning side he scored a lucky seven times over 45 appearances. Following a long line of quality players being transferred just as City show signs of success, Mike went to Oxford in 1988 for £150,000 after hitting the net 13 times over 145 appearances. He rejoined the club in '98 and by the following season was team captain.

Trevor FORD

"I never thought I would join Cardiff City..."
A dynamite goal-scorer in the number 9 shirt, Ford made a name for himself both on and off

the pitch during a playing career that included Cardiff, Sunderland, Swansea and Newport County. A full Welsh inter-national with 38 caps Ford plied his trade in the North east and at Aston Villa prior to arriving at Ninian Park. It was whilst playing for the Swans against Villa that he hit a hat trick with a transfer fee of £100,000 being paid for his services resulting in his move to Villa Park. Signed by Cardiff City as a replacement for Alf Sherwood, he scored 12 goals in his first season of 1956/ 1957 and is remembered as a stern hitter of the ball. Able to use both feet, the 'fire-brand' and Swansea-born lad possessed dark looks and a blitzkrieg-type strength strategy. Not only that, he was not shy in speaking his mind. When a Cardiff player, Ford refused to play out of position and would not accept a contract for less than £15 a week. He believed that established professionals should be valued and that they be selected in their established position on the field. His earthy comments were given full vent in his tasty autobiography I Lead the Attack! Its revelations led to Ford being suspended from playing. As a Sunderland player, Trevor represented Wales in the international v England at Ninian Park in 1952 amongst a number of international appearances which saw him strike 23 goals. In three seasons with City he collected 5 Wales caps and in all netted 59 times over 119 appearances. He later briefly Newport County following a lengthy period plying his trade in the Netherlands after leaving Cardiff. Trevor Ford was awarded the PFA medal in 1999 as part of their 100 Legends of League Football roll call. He died in 2003 aged 79.

Jason FOWLER

Scored through a marvellous chip over the Brentford 'keeper that left 3 players ball watching. Fowler's goal was one of the four scored by City in a 4-1 win at Ninian Park in January 1999. His became one of the many goals scored at the ground that will forever be lauded. Bristol-born like another former Bluebird, Mike Ford, Jason came to the club from Bristol City in a 1996 transfer. Last known to be playing for Torquay United.

Gerry FRANCIS

A former England captain as a player and as both with a strong link to Q.P.R. Francis came to City at the tail end of his playing career when Jimmy Goodfellow was in charge. He made seven consecutive appearances on a non-contract basis after arriving as a recent player-manager of Exeter City: a final two when Alan Durban helmed the Bluebirds. Gerry made his home debut in a 2-4 defeat by Brighton. All in all, his career at City records as played in seven and lost six. Replaced by Brian Flynn, another player in the twilight of his playing days. Francis moved on and made half as many appearances in a Swansea City shirt. Gerry had played for Q.P.R v City back in the early-70s at Ninian Park as well as for Exeter much later.

Robin FRIDAY

'As a footballer, Robin had everything.' Stan Bowles, Goal magazine, March 1996.'I can picture him now, long hair flowing, cutting in from the wing, beating 2 or 3 players. He really was outstanding. His ball control was absolutely fabulous -I've never seen anything like it.' Former Cardiff City Doctor, Dr Leslie Hamilton. A true individual with a great flair for football to boot. Friday was bought as a striker replacement for then recently-departed Adrian Alston. Robin arrived after Mike England and Alston had left to join the blossoming soccer league in America. Signed from Reading in December '76 for £30,000, and still held as a legendary player at that club, Friday made his debut at Ninian Park in a 3-0 win v Fulham on New Year's day as sports writer Karl Woodward recorded in the Echo match report. Despite his 6' height, Robin would consistently be victimized by opposing players so much so that even City boss Jimmy Andrews acknowledged. In the Fulham game Friday gave former England captain Bobby Moore the run around all afternoon and both he and opponent John Lacey were involved in 'heated exchanges' with the new Bluebird.

At one stage he was said to have grabbed Mr Moore in a very intimate area! Robin hit a stunning second goal, a shot struck with the outside of his right boot. In a match against Charlton he received a fractured cheekbone, which resulted in him missing some

games. A classic example that sums up the spirit of Robin Friday presented itself in a league match at Ninian Park on 1 August 1977. City won 4-2 after a personal battle had been fought between the visitors' goalkeeper, Milija Aleksic and Friday. The City player scored twice and Robin stuck his two fingers up to the floored 'keeper as he ran off to celebrate. Aleksic had a torrid afternoon in a fixture seen by 10,460 spectators. The image was captured beautifully by Echo photographer Dave Jones. Friday was subsequently suspended for the next 2 matches but not by the referee who missed the gesture entirely! 'I am not a villain. But I do get involved because I am a winner.' Acknowledge the crowds applause he then stuck his fingers up to keeper. 'I can't remember doing that.' He pronounced in the Echo 18/4/1977. Welsh band the Super Furry Animals utilize the famous Jones photograph on the cover of their single, The Man Don't Give A F**k. Friday was voted the Reading Player of the Millennium in 1999. He scored 53 goals in 135 games at Elm Park. For reasons unknown, Robin left Ninian Park in December of that Jubilee year after less than 25 appearances as a Bluebird. He died in 1990.

Danny GABBIDON

'I like classy footballers and he is one of those, he is a natural.'

Mickey Thomas, former Wales international. One of the classiest defenders to come out of Ninian Park Danny came to the club from West Brom where he was a trainee. A total of 26 appearances followed before his loan spell with the Bluebirds was subsequently made permanent by a bargain fee of £175,00. An ever-present on the City team sheet since 2000. Gabbidon has developed in to a rotund international for Wales and was excellent in the World Cup qualifying match v England in October 2004. Speculation mounts about his future despite his signing of a new contract with Cardiff in 2004.

Roger GIBBINS

'The basic point about my game is that I am an attacking player...but I'm not too proud to claim them from anywhere- chest, knee...they all count!' The moustachioed 'Gibbo' seemed to collect clubs as a player including Cardiff and Swansea and following the conclusion of his outfield career, he managed Merthyr Tydfil for a time. As did Eddie May, John Charles and Colin Addison. With football being a small world, Roger was in the Swans side that beat Cardiff 2-0 in a 1986 league match at the Vetch Field. The Bluebirds were relegated that season and three years later Gibbins was back as a City player. Originally coming to Ninian Park on a free transfer, he made his debut v Wrexham on the opening day of the 1982/ 1983 season and is an ever-present. Some 160 appearances in a blue shirt followed until a move to Swansea City is created and he moves up to the Vetch in an exchange deal. March 1989 sees his return and 31 goals have his name on them in 271 additional appearances.

David GILES

'What he, and others must realize is that I do not pick the teams. Every player who wears the club shirt in a league match has picked

himself. That's why he is there.' A bizarre piece of hokum from City boss Jimmy Andrews after turning down an early transfer request by Giles, seen opposite, in 1975. Cardiff born and bred, David signed for Cardiff as a schoolboy back in 1974. He and his brother, also a City player, were brought up in the same area as John Toshack and Leighton James, both fellow Welsh internationals. During his two spells at the club in 1974-1978 and 1985-1986 respectively, Giles gathered 12 Welsh caps. 'Gilo' was a Welsh schoolboy international prior to breaking in to the Cardiff first-team where he made 70 appearances and scored 10 times. A transfer to Wrexham in 1978, three years after his Ninian Park debut v Notts Forest, was succeeded by a fruitful period at Swansea and a healthy build up of Welsh caps. He played against his former club at Ninian Park whilst a Crystal Palace player. Giles returned to Cardiff City once more in September 1985 [he had been a Newport player over the 1984 season]with 134 additional appearances recorded. He eventually left for a move to Barry Town and once again played against the Bluebirds in a Welsh Cup tie. Over the course of his footballing career, David was to play for all 4 Welsh league clubs. His brother was also a City and Newport County man. Both siblings were involved with Merthyr Tydfil in the mid-1990s, David as a coach and brother Paul as a player. He now makes his mark as a radio football pundit with Real Radio and columnist with the local newspaper, both of which cause much controversy with fans!

Jimmy GILL

Scored twice on his debut for the Bluebirds in his and City's first league game, a 5-2 away defeat at Stockport County. City still managed to win promotion over that 1920/ 1921 season and in his time in Wales he scored a brace of hat-tricks and made the selection for the 1925 FA Cup final. His departure came in the following season with his playing record set out as: 103 goals/ 220 games.

Jimmy GILLIGAN

Signing from Lincoln City in 1987, the 6'2" Gilligan had seen mixed success as a player before joining Cardiff City in 1987 following a loan spell with Newport County. His luck soon changed as he scored the only goal on his home debut in a 1-1 draw v Orient. He also popped in a further goal in the championship-winning season for the Bluebirds. An ever-present in the 1987/ 1988 season Jimmy scored twice as Cardiff won the Welsh Cup against Wrexham. Jimmy left the Bluebirds in the 1989/ 1990 season when he completed a move to Portsmouth where a certain Frank Burrows was then manager. As a Swansea player, Gilligan scored the winner in their 2-1 FA Cup victory against his old club in November 1991. He was promoted to manager of the recently formed MK Dons in mid-2004.

Gavin GORDON

Played in the City side that beat Leeds United in that famous 2-1 FA Cup victory at Ninian Park in 2001. Now at Notts County and still scoring.

Grange END

"I used to enjoy a visit to Ninian Park," recounts Bristol supporter Anthony Killbe, "until it was like a cage on match days when Rovers were playing there. Some of the banter was ok but on other occasions a bit choice. " Swansea City follower, Ron Richards, saw a derby match when both sides were in Division Two, "On both the way in and out of the ground we had to be protected by a police cordon from being attacked by Cardiff fans. The away end was at that time open to the elements and a -

particularly unpleasant place to be." The John Smiths Grange End was originally constructed in 1928 and has been modernized quite a bit since then. Thankfully, a cover was added to enable up to 18,000 supporters shelter and opened on 28 September for the home game v Burnley, which City won. Away fans are segregated by a dividing line known as No Man's Land, which keeps a distance from the vociferous City fans opposite. Strangely, fans can also sit in front of the away enclosure too. Vickie Parker, visited Ninian Park with her then boyfriend, an avid Bluebirds fan, for a Port Vale fixture a few years ago, "I stood in the Grange end, where the Vale fans were in easy reach and the amount of rubbish thrown over the dividing fence was astounding, but the Vale fans weren't too nice either. The Grange caused problems for me because the steps aren't very high in height difference and being short, I found it difficult to see over those in front of me...the club will always be special to me." So not all feedback has been negative from visiting fans, take Bristolian Di Rowlands, "The last few visits have not been to friendly but they [Cardiff] have the best burgers going."

Wilf GRANT

A cultured centre forward that netted goals for City in a number of games, of particular importance being a brace v Leeds United in a promotion-seeking season. Moving from Southampton, Wilf was originally used as winger before a stroke of luck saw him used as a striker. He and Cardiff never looked back and he soon started knocking the goals in; including

a hat trick in the semi-finals of the Welsh Cup in 1954. He would sign off as a Cardiff City player in the 7-1 away defeat at Preston where he scored the single City goal. Wilf made 169 first-team starts with 73 goals collected. He returned in 1958 as part of the Ninian Park coaching staff assisting manager Bill Jennings. Grant was considered by many as being the driving force at CCFC during that period. He passed away in 1990.

Peter GROTIER

Goalkeeper who enjoyed two periods at Cardiff, 40 appearances gathered in his second spell in the 1979/ 1980 season onwards. In addition, Peter played in a couple of games on loan in '73. He was in and out of the side competing with City legend Ron Healey for the number 1 shirt, and later had the additional challenge from teen-aged Andy Dibble. He left at the end of the '81/' 82 season.

Sam HAMMAM

The eccentric, Lebanon-born Mr Hammam took control of Cardiff City Football Club in August 2000. His football history as a chairman was underlined with great success achieved at Wimbledon F.C and the legendary 'Crazy Gang' featuring the likes of Dennis Wise, Alan Cork and Vinnie Jones. It was that side that beat Liverpool in the 1988 FA Cup Final a mere 7 years since Sam became the owner and chairman of the Dons.

Billy HARDY

A shiny-domed City stalwart known around the grounds of the football league in the 1920s for his appearance alone, having gone prematurely bold. He began his Cardiff career during the 1926/ 1927 season after being brought to the club by Fred Stewart from Stockport County. The Bluebirds won the Cup for their first and only time in 1927 despite the fact that they had been forced to play 4 games in as many days. As a City player, Hardy helped win the Welsh Cup in 1928 and 1930 and played in the 1956 final v Swansea Town seen by 37,500 at Ninian Park. City took the honours following a 3-2 win. A quiet, unassuming character much like Len Davies, Bluebirds manager Fred Stewart termed him "a wonderful left-back." Billy played for the club more than 400 times over 11 years. Strangely, it was said that he was not capped for England due to playing for a Welsh club. Whatever, the charismatic Mr Hardy made his last appearance in a City shirt v Gillingham in a 1-0 in March 1932. He died in 1981.

Alan HARRINGTON

Born locally Alan won 11 Wales caps and played in the blue shirt on more than 400 occasions. His debut came in a 0-0 with Spurs in 1952. He had joined City as a part-timer in 1951 before a broken leg curtailed his career in 1966.

Bob HATTON

'If I can score the goals that take us back into the Second Division, that's my mission.'
As a weathered 36-year-old centre forward Hatton arrived at Cardiff in the midst of the 1981/82 season. He had been working as an insurance broker in Sheffield and would play for the club as a part-timer. During the 1969/ 1970 season and in the following one, he played against City for his then-third club, Carlisle United. Bob had been on the opposing side at Ninian Park in a 2-2 draw with Blackpool back in the '76/ '77 season [the City favourite scored twice that afternoon]. Eclipsed by all this, was a hat trick collected v Cardiff City in October '77. He wore a Luton Town shirt in numerous taskforces sent to Ninian Park too. He also nabbed one of the 4 goals netted during a pre-season friendly at City in July 1976. After Cardiff had gained promotion over the season that he was playing here, Bob Hatton retired from football in May 1983 after more than 600 games and 200+ goals scored. Bluebirds manager Len Ashurst had brought him to the club and he himself moved on in August 1983.

Ron HEALEY

This Liverpool-born goalkeeper signed for Cardiff in March 1974 and played until injury ended his career in 1981. Previously playing for his home town club and Manchester City, where he was overshadowed by the might of Joe

Corrigan, Ron was an almighty walloper of the ball and as a child, I would watch it fly down towards the Grange End. A great presence for the Bluebirds, Healey gained the first of two international caps for the Republic of Ireland v Poland, in 1977. Eire were then managed by former Leeds United hard man Johnny Giles who had played at Ninian Park against City in 1964 and in the 1971/72 season. Attended by 49,180, United beat City by two goals that afternoon. Ron once made a priceless last-minute save in a 1-1 away game v Swansea City that kept the Bluebirds in Division Two. In all, he played at Ninian Park across six seasons, accumulating 267 first-team games. His loyalty was acknowledged by City when he was awarded a testimonial match v Wolves in the 1983/ 1984 season.

Jeff HEMMERMAN

"He gets the ball an' scores a goal - Jeffrey Hemmerman" City chant. A big City favourite hitting the net some 22 times whilst in the club colours. Jeff was a major success in the promotion-winning team of 1982/ 1983. In fact, Jeff scored his first goal against City for his hometown club Hull City in a 1-1 draw back in the '76/'77 season. Hemmerman began his goalscoring spree for the Bluebirds v Sheffield United in front of 7,147. His last strike being in the 4-1 battering of Southend United at Ninian Park in April 1983. Sadly, injury put paid to his playing career and he now works as a physiotherapist.

Gerry HITCHENS

A 'chunky centre-forward', well-respected by former City striker Trevor Ford when writing in his autobiography I Lead the Attack! Hitchens came to City for £1,500 from hometown club Kidderminster and immediately joined up with former Villa striker Ford. He made his home debut in April 1955 v Wolves in a 2-3 defeat. Gerry scored 5 times in a single match, the semi-final of the Welsh Cup v Oswestry, which saw Cardiff on their way to winning the trophy in 1956. Playing at Ninian Park until 1957 he had employment outside of the game at Nantgarw Colliery. In total, he appeared 108 times in a City shirt and put in 57 goals for the club. His career continued after his time with the Bluebirds including a Division Two championship medal with Aston Villa, a successful spell with 3 Italian clubs (one being Inter Milan) and finally with the less-glamorous sides of Worchester and Merthyr Tydfil. Gerry died whilst playing in a charity match in 1983.

Barry HOLE

As a wing-half he started his career at Cardiff in 1959 and ended it at Swansea in 1971. [pictured opposite]

Ken HOLLYMAN

'On his day perhaps one of

the most brilliant players in the game.' A Cardiff lad, Hollyman featured in the post-war side that was selected to play against Dinamo Moscow in 1945. The Welsh international scored 10 goals in the Division Two season campaign of 1948/ 1949, netting the only goals in two consecutive 1-0 victories v Plymouth and Tottenham Hotspur. Ken possessed one of the longest throw-ins of his day ala Andy Legg. Upon leaving Ninian Park in November 1953, and despite an injury, Ken enjoyed seven seasons with Newport County and as player/manager with Ton Pentre. A Bluebird 129 times and on a further 81 occasions during the war years.

Godfrey INGRAM

'Lovely skills, lovely touches. There was fear in some defenders' eyes.' Luton Town manager

David Pleat, 1982. An England Schoolboy international, Ingram was playing in the U.S Soccer League in 1981 when a City announced their plans to pay £200,000 for his services the following year. Ingram, twenty at the time, was in the Luton Town squad that came to City in the '81/ '82 season but he didn't feature. His stay at Ninian Park is recorded at a mere 9 weeks after which time he rejoined San Jose Earthquakes for the exact same fee [he had been palmed out on

loan at Aberdeen and Northampton and played for the New York Cosmos]. Whilst with the Bluebirds he managed to get on the score sheet twice; hitting the winner against Gillingham.

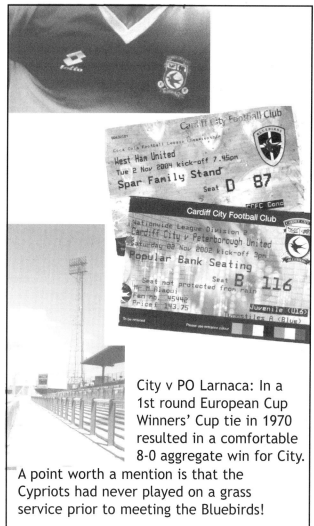

City v PO Larnaca: In a 1st round European Cup Winners' Cup tie in 1970 resulted in a comfortable 8-0 aggregate win for City. A point worth a mention is that the Cypriots had never played on a grass service prior to meeting the Bluebirds!

For a great many years Ninian Park served as the home ground for Welsh international matches. Swansea's Vetch Field and Wrexham's Racecourse Ground have also been used and of course, the Millennium Stadium now facilitates all of the games. The Arms Park has been documented as being the location for a small number of fixtures prior to the very first international to be staged at Ninian Park in 1896.

Wales were thrashed 1-9.

Many matches have since been fought out since with visitors including Czechoslovakia, Brazil, Spain, Italy, Israel, USSR, Hungary, Iceland, Ireland, East Germany, Yugoslavia, Uruguay, Denmark, Costa Rica, Italy and Rumania. In February 1958, Wales sealed their subsequent appearance in the World Cup Finals [held that time in Sweden] by beating Israel 2-0 at Ninian Park. England and Scotland have visited on numerous occasions and featured on the next few pages are a few of the key remembered games.

Wales v England MATCHES

Wales have met the 'Old Enemy' as Ivor Allchurch called them, some 26 times at City's club ground since that first meeting back in 1896. Wales have not fared at all well in these meetings; with one win recorded up until the last time the countries met there in April 1982 which saw a 0-1 England win. An astronomical 54,000 were at Ninian Park in 1938 to enjoy the two countries play in a match that the Welsh won by 4-2.

15/10/ 1949 - A mighty crowd of 61,079 see the English win 4-1 with Jackie Milburn collecting a hat trick during the period when City's Ninian Park ground was well-established as the home of Welsh football.

10/10/1953 - Wales were again beaten 1-4 despite having John Charles and Trevor Ford turning out for them.

22/10/1955 - 'One of the greatest full-backs Wales has ever produced.' Appertaining to ex-City skipper Alf Sherwood the programme notes proved a cool prognosis. Sherwood was in action as a man-marker of Tom Finney with Trevor Ford also in the Welsh side. Wales had not beaten the English for seventeen years but on this day they won 2-1 with future-Bluebird Derek Tapscott scoring one of the red goals.

17/10/ 1959 - A 1-1 draw made noteworthy in that the scorer for Wales that day was a Cardiff City player, Graham Moore. The cost of a programme for the game was one shilling.

The last time the sides had met in Cardiff saw England hammer the Welsh 0-4 in October '57 with a goal from Tom Finney.

14/10/1961 - Brothers John and Mel Charles play in the Welsh first eleven. One Bobby Robson is in the England side whilst the Welsh team features 2 Cardiff players. A record attendance of 61,566 are present that day.

Jimmy Scoular

12/10/1963 - Wales 0 v England 4. Neither Ivor Allchurch or Mel and John Charles could stem defeat that day. England's team included Jimmy Greaves, Bobby Moore and Bobby Charlton. Two further draws were recorded at Ninian Park over the next two decades with the last meeting at the ground in 1982.

5/05/1972 & 15/11/1972 - Both 1-0 wins for the visitors.

Wales v Scotland matches

Scotland first came to Ninian Park in March 1903 taking away a 0-1 win. Subsequently, 23 further matches have been played there between the two nations. September 1985 saw the last fixture to be held at the Cardiff ground with the result that day being 1-1.

18/10/1952 - Wales 1 Scotland 2: Arthur 'Buller' Lever and Fred Stansfield both turn out for Wales as present and previous Cardiff City players respectively. Oddly, it was to be both men's only cap with Lever having a tough time marking Kop idol Billy Liddell. Billy had scored in a previous international meeting between the countries in a 3-1 October 1950 win for the Scots. Trevor Ford, then a Sunderland striker, turns out for Wales. Future City boss Jimmy Scoular won the 2nd of his nine full international caps for Scotland as a Portsmouth player.

18/10/1958 - Sir Matt Busby was the Scottish national manager at the time as well as being Manchester United boss. It was not long after the Munich air disaster of February '58, which resulted in the deaths of many of the United first team. Wales were then managed Jimmy Murphy, Matt's Old Trafford assistant. Denis Law made his full international debut as an eighteen-year-old, becoming the youngest player to be capped by Scotland. He was learning his trade at Huddersfield Town at the time. The Wales team had the likes of John Charles and Ivor Allchurch in it, which had returned from reaching the quarter-finals of the World Cup that summer. Wales were soundly beaten 0-3 and future Man United legend Law inadvertently got his name on the score sheet after the ball rebounded in off him and in to the goal. Tommy Docherty is in the Scottish team alongside the aforementioned Law. Two years previously the Scots had defeated Wales 1-0 also at Ninian Park.

20/10/1962 - Wales 2 v

Scotland 3: Denis Law scores for the Scots whilst the Charles brothers are in opposition. A Cardiff City player broke his leg in a challenge with Law in a '61 match.

1966 - Wales 1 v Scotland 1: The game was played in a somber atmosphere having occurred a day after the Aberfan tragedy. A large blanket was carried around the pitch at half time with fans tossing coins to contribute to the rescue fund. "I was only twelve," remembers Laurence New, "and it was a bit of a crush leaving the ground among about 33,000 fans. But it was worth it despite the weather." Writing in his autobiography, Denis Law, who scored that day, concedes that the eventual draw hardly registered. Forever remembered for a cheeky back-heeler which sent his former club down in to Division Two, made perfect by the fact that he was a Man City player at the time!

Bill IRWIN
A good City keeper from the early 1970s who was put straight in to the first team almost immediately upon his arrival at Ninian Park. He made his home Cardiff debut in a 1-2 defeat by Millwall in the 1971/ 1972 campaign. A home crowd of 17,931 were there to see the debut of this Irish 20 year-old. Hailing from Bangor, Billy battled with Ron Healey for the number one shirt from the '73 season through to the 1977/ '78 season

campaign. He completed 210 appearances as City goalkeeper before leaving for the American Soccer League in the guise of Washington Diplomats.

Leighton JAMES
A left-winger born in Wales back in 1953. James made his name as a pro with Burnley, Derby & Q.P.R before signing for Swansea City in 1980. He was the top-scorer at the Vetch in their Division Two promotion-winning side. Played briefly in the player-coach role at Newport whilst eventually managing South Wales club Llanelli.

Robbie JAMES.
Arrived from Bradford City as the latest addition to the Cardiff City squad for the upcoming 1992/ 1993 season, of which he was to be an ever-present. At the end of that campaign he was awarded the Player of the Season mantle and was also commemorated as Man of the Match for a local

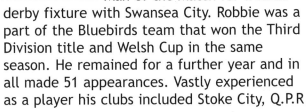

derby fixture with Swansea City. Robbie was a part of the Bluebirds team that won the Third Division title and Welsh Cup in the same season. He remained for a further year and in all made 51 appearances. Vastly experienced as a player his clubs included Stoke City, Q.P.R and Leicester not to mention his Welsh international and club connections! His final match in a Cardiff shirt was the away game at York City in October 1993. It was as a Swan that his record is truly special though, playing as he did in 394 games and scoring 99 goals over a ten-year period. James continued to play and knock in the occasion goal for Merthyr Tydfil [as player/manager], Barry Town and Llanelli. However, tragically he died of a heart attack whilst playing for Llanelli in February 1998. He played in 782 matches, netting 133 goals.

Linden JONES

This short and stocky City defender [seen above]that played for the City from 1978 through to mid-way in the 1983/ 1984 season, gathering

a little over 160 appearances and three goals. He was in the Bluebirds side relegated in 1981/ 1982 and missed only three games in the promotion-winning side of the following season. His home debut arrived v Leyton Orient in front of 8,239 in February 1979. Jones continued the line of Cardiff City full backs progressing to full Welsh international

status playing as he did in that balmy Wales friendly v Brazil watched by 35,000 at Ninian Park. He left City in September 1983 and joined Somerton Park's Newport County for 4 seasons. Linden was most recently working for local rivals Swansea City.

Graham KAVANAGH

'The fans today again were a different class. They made it sound like a home game. They really do get behind us.'

Kavanagh after scoring in the 2-3 victory away at Wolves, September 2004. Lennie Lawrence gave 'Kav' his league debut when in charge at Middlesborough. Graham scored for 'Boro in a 1993/ 1994 season FA Cup replay which Cardiff won away. Dublin-born and full Republic of Ireland international Graham's previous clubs also include Darlington and Stoke City. He came to Cardiff in the summer of 2001 with a million pound price tag but has proved a worthy investment as the City captain with a penchant for a volley. It was Alan Cork who brought Kav to Ninian Park and his investment was justified with the Irish man scoring the City goal in a 1-1 debut v Peterborough in mid 2001.

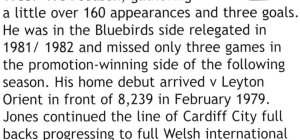

Kevin KEELAN

Played numerous times at Ninian Park v City and against the Bluebirds at Carrow road. New City signing John Charles scored a freaky goal against Keelan on his debut at City's ground in the 1963/ 1964 season. Keelan was regarded as one of the best outside of the First Division in his day. He kept goal for the Canaries in a 0-0 at Ninian in the

71/ 72 season that saw upcoming Bluebird Doug Livermore in their side.

Fred KEENOR

A City half back synonymous as the Bluebirds captain that

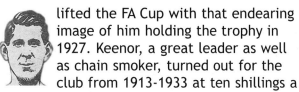

lifted the FA Cup with that endearing image of him holding the trophy in 1927. Keenor, a great leader as well as chain smoker, turned out for the club from 1913-1933 at ten shillings a week. Former City manager Fred Stewart interviewed in 1924, said of the Wales and City captain, '...sums up the attitude of our club. I honestly do not believe that the word 'beaten' is in his vocabulary.' The jug-eared Mr Keenor saw active service in WWII, suffering wounds to both his shoulder and knees. An incredibly fit athlete despite the smoking, Keenor was well-thought of by the Bob Bank faithful due to his absolute demand of high standards from not only himself but for the good of the team. He played his final game in a City shirt in a goal-less match against Spurs at Ninian Park in April 1931. Another City favourite, Len Davies, also made his farewell appearance that day. Although wanted by other clubs during his career Keenor remained at the club for 19 years. He moved on to Crewe Alexander,

making more than 100 appearances prior to returning to play non-league. Born in 1894 he died in 1972 after returning to Cardiff in 1958 to work as a labourer! His son, Graham, was involved with the admin side of the club for many years in the 60s/ 70s.

Peter KING

'Speedy attacker and tireless worker.' [pictured opposite]
The slightly-built 'King Machine'

scored 108 goals for City over 13 seasons with the club accumulating 469 appearances before injury curtailed his playing career. Born in Worcester where he played his club football prior to coming to Cardiff, Peter unfortunately missed the majority of the '62/ '63 campaign at Ninian Park after arriving in 1961. His debut came in a Division One match v Burnley in October '61. Highlights include his two strikes in the Welsh cup final v Bangor City, netting the Bluebirds first European Cup Winners' Cup goal v Esbjerg and being the top scorer in the 1967/ 1968 season. He and John Toshack both struck hat tricks in a Welsh Cup tie with Ebbw Vale; wonder who got to keep the ball?

Peter KITCHEN

A prolific goal scorer who joined Cardiff City in 1980 from Fulham. He made his full debut against another former club, Leyton Orient in August '82, the same season that would see him finish top scorer. Peter knocked in five goals in a Welsh Cup game v Cardiff Corinthians, which the Bluebirds won easily by 6-0. In addition, in the 1981/ 1982 relegation season for City, he hit a hat-trick against Wrexham. Peter left Cardiff for a spell in Hong Kong and then re-joined Orient.

Les LEA

Born in Manchester, Lea came to Cardiff in 1967 and made his debut v Bolton. Les went on to score 16 times over his 98 starts.

Cardiff City's League positioning 2004/ 2005 season - 1910/ 1911

2004/2005 Coca-Cola Championship -   2003/2004 Nationwide League Division One - 13th 2002/2003 Nationwide League Division Two - 6th 2001/ 2002 Nationwide League Division Two - 4th 2000/ 2001 Nationwide League Division Three - 2nd 1999/ 2000 Nationwide League Division Two - 21st 1998/ 1999 Nationwide League Division Three - 3rd 1997/ 1998 Nationwide League Division Two - 21st 1996/ 1997 Nationwide League Division Two - 7th 1995/ 1996 Endsleigh League Division Three - 22nd 1994/ 1995 Endsleigh League Division Two - 22nd 1993/ 1994 Endsleigh League Division Three - 19th 1992/ 1993 Endsleigh League Division Two - 1st 1991/ 1992 Barclays Fourth Division - 9th 1990/ 1991Barclays Fourth Division - 13th 1989/1990 Barclays Third Division - 21st 1988/1989 Barclays Third Division - 16th 1987/1988 Barclays Fourth Division - 2nd 1986/ 1987 Today Fourth Division - 13th 1985/ 1986 Canon Third Division - 22nd 1984/ 1985 Canon Second Division - 21st 1983/ 1984 Canon Second Division - 14th 1982/ 1983 English Third Division - 2nd 1981/ 1982 Second Division - 20th 1980/ 1981 Second Division - 19th 1979/ 1980 Second Division - 15th 1978/ 1979 Second Division - 9th 1977/ 1978 Second Division - 19th 1976/ 1977 Second Division - 18th 1975/ 1976 Third Division - 2nd 1974/ 1975 Second Division - 21st 1973/ 1974 Second Division - 17th 1972/ 1973 Second Division - 20th 1971/ 1972 Second Division - 19th 1970/ 1971 Second Division - 3rd 1969/ 1970 Second Division - 7th 1968/ 1969 Second Division - 5th 1967/ 1968 Second Division - 13th 1966/ 1967 Second Division - 20th 1965/ 1966 Second Division - 20th 1964/1965 Second Division - 13th 1963/ 1964 Second Division - 15th 1962/ 1963 Second Division - 10th 1961/ 1962 First Division - 21st 1960/ 1961 First Division - 15th 1959/ 1960 Second Division - 2nd 1958/ 1959 Second Division - 9th 1957/ 1958 Second Division - 15th 1956/ 1957 First Division - 21st 1955/ 1956 First Division - 17th 1954/ 1955 First Division - 20th 1953/ 1954 First Division - 10th 1952/ 1953 First Division - 12th 1951/ 1952 Second Division - 2nd 1950/ 1951 Second Division - 3rd 1949/ 1950 Second Division - 10th 1948/ 1949 Second Division - 4th 1947/ 1948 Second Division - 5th 1946/1947 Third Division (South) - 1st 1938/ 1939 Third Division (South) - 13th 1937/ 1938 Third Division (South) - 10th 1936/ 1937 Third Division (South) - 18th 1935/ 1936 Third Division (South) - 20th 1934/ 1935 Third Division (South) - 19th 1933/ 1934 Third Division (South) - 22nd 1932/ 1933 Third Division (South) - 19th 1931/ 1932 Third Division (South) - 9th 1930/ 1931 Second Division - 22nd 1929/ 1930 Second Division - 8th 1928/ 1929 First Division - 22nd 1927/ 1928 First Division - 6th 1926/ 1927 First Division - 14th 1925/ 1926 First Division - 16th 1924/ 1925 First Division - 11th 1923/ 1924 First Division - 2nd 1922/ 1923 First Division - 9th 1921/ 1922 First Division - 4th 1920/ 1921 Second Division - 2nd

Cardiff City v Leeds United matches over the years

[City] "...a fair to middling 2nd Division team."
So commented Guardian journalist David Lacey, writing before Cardiff's stupendous 2-1 FA Cup victory over Leeds on 6th January 2002. Australian Mark Viduka worked relentlessly for the visitors and put them ahead sometime after Gavin Gordon had put Rio Ferdinand out of the game with a heavy challenge that saw the England youngster hobble off. Graham Kavanagh, such a majestic presence in a City shirt, equalized from a free kick and Leeds were never going to leave the ground with a victory from this moment on. Alan Smith, as with Ferdinand, has since moved on to bigger things with Manchester United, and his sending off gave a tremendous boost to both the Bluebirds and the home crowd. A goal mouth scramble involving Leo Fortune West resulting in the winning goal from Cardiff lad Scott Young.

Over the seasons City have met Leeds in a number of cup and league games with mainly positive results. In the 2004/ 2005 season City and Leeds drew 0-0 at Ninian Park in a Division Two match watched by 17,006. It was some one thousand days since the epic FA Cup tie of January 2002 where the Bluebirds humbled the Championship leaders. Below is a further selection of the most interesting meetings between the sides.

3 May 1952 - Cardiff City 3 v Leeds 1

51,000 souls were there on a rainy afternoon made significant in that City needed to win their last three games to gain promotion as runners-up in Division Two. The Bluebirds had beaten Blackburn and Bury and continued in the same vein this afternoon. Leeds featured Bobby and Jack Charlton's uncle, Jackie Milburn, in their side that day.

FA CUP 3rd round - 7 January 1956
Leeds 1 City 2
With a Leeds side that included John Charles, 45,000 were at Elland road for this Cup tie. Almost postponed until the fog lifted, City had recently beaten the then-mighty Wolves whilst Leeds were unbeaten at home in their last 32 matches. Trevor Ford and Gerry Hitchens worked well together for City.

FA Cup 3rd round - 4/01/1964
City 0 Leeds 1
Billy Bremner scores the winner at Ninian in amongst a team brimming with sheer quality. However, City were to hold them to 1-1 in a league fixture soon after.

League match - 26/02/1972
City 0 Leeds 2
Johnny Giles scored both goals for the

visitors in a first 11 which numbered Charlton/ Hunter/ Lorimar and Clarke.

FA Cup - 6/01/2002

City 2 Leeds 1

A stupendous victory by the Bluebirds, a Second Division club at the time when their opponents including the likes of Robbie Fowler, Danny Mills and Lee Bowyer, were atop of the Premiership. The sides had last met back in a 1984 Division Two fixture which Cardiff won 2-1 at Ninian Park. 22,009 see John Charles, a player in his career for both teams, presented before the kick off as the special guest.

Coca-Cola Championship - October 2004

0-0 at Ninian Park

Andy LEGG

'I've never seen such raw commitment.' Ex-City midfielder Paul Millar.

Signed for Cardiff as a schoolboy and never gave less than 100%, be it running all over the pitch or producing one of his legendary throw-ins, 1989/ 1990 was his first season as a Bluebird. Steadily building up his total of appearances, peaking at 42 in the 1999/ 2000 campaign, he scored 8 goals for the club in a 5 year stay. On loan at the Vetch Filed, Andy played against Cardiff City along with ex-City player Jimmy Gilligan. He spent two seasons with the Swans in the early-1990s and finally departed from Ninian Park during the summer of 2003 at which time he became a player-coach with Peterborough United. He had previously spent a little time with the Posh on loan there back in 1998.

Arthur 'Buller' LEVER

A fast right back who joined City in 1943 from a local side. In a service career of 156 appearances, and ever-present in seasons 1946-47 and 1947-48, Buller was transferred to Leicester City in 1950. By the 54/55 season he was back in the principality with Newport County and was to return to Ninian Park as a Welsh international playing v Scotland in 1948. His death in 2004 was marked in Cardiff newspapers.

Steve LYNEX

The midlands-born Lynex came to Ninian on a free transfer from West Brom, making his debut in a 1-2 defeat by Fulham. Previously carving out a name for himself in a Leicester side with a young Gary Lineker in it, Lynex played at City alongside Lineker in the 1981/ 1982 season. He even took over goalkeeping duties for his former club during a game v Shrewsbury. Steve played 82 times for the Bluebirds and nabbed 4 goals in a 2 seasons spell.

Danny MALLOY

'Hard as nails but he could also play.' Colin Baker, former team mate. He came to City following the retirement of Stan Montgomery in 1955. His debut v Charlton, is remembered for a hat-trick scored by Bluebird Neil O'Halloran. Danny, signed from Dundee, had the unenviable task of man-marking John Charles in a 1956 Cup tie at Leeds. He did a grand job in front of a 40,000 crowd and Cardiff won 2-1.

Cyril Spiers

Alan Durban

Bill Jones

Trevor Morris

MANAGERS	Present to first
Lennie LAWRENCE	February 2002 - still...
Alan CORK	July 2001 - February 2002
Bobby GOULD	August 2000 - July 2001
Billy AYRE	February 2000 - August 2000
Frank BURROWS	February 1998 - February 2000
Kenny HIBBITT	January 1998 - February 1998
Phil NEAL	August 1996 - July 1996
Eddie MAY	March 1995 - May 1995
Terry YORATH	August 1994 - March 1995
Eddie MAY	July 1991 - November 1994
Len ASHURST	August 1989 - May 1991
Frank BURROWS	May 1986 - August 1999
Alan DURBAN	September 1984 - May 1986
Jimmy GOODFELLOW	March 1984 - September 1984
Len ASHURST	March 1982 - March 1984
Graham WILLIAMS	November 1981 - February 1982
Richie MORGAN	November 1978 - March 1981
Jimmy ANDREWS	May 1974 - November 1978
Frank O'FARRELL	November 1973 - April 1974
Jimmy SCOULAR	June 1964 - November 1973
George SWINDIN	October 1962 - April 1964
Bill JONES	September 1958 - Sept 1962
Trevor MORRIS	April 1954 - August 1958
Cyril SPIERS	April 1948 - April 1954
Bill MCCANDLESS	June 1946 - November 1948
Cyril SPIERS	April 1939 - April 1946
Bill JENNINGS	April 1937 - April 1939
Ben WATTS-JONES	February 1934 - April 1937
Bart Wilson	May 1933 - February 1934
Fred STEWART	May 1911 - May 1933
Davy MCDOUGALL	August 1910 - May 1911

Frank O'Farrell

Jimmy Scoular

Trevor Morris

Alan Cork

Frank Burrows

Davy MCDOUGALL

City's first professional captain as a player in 1910 and in a player-manager role in 1911. As a previous Bristol City and Glasgow Rangers pro, Big Mac shaped a team consisting mainly of non-Welshmen with 14 professional players and some amateurs to select from. Mr McDougall managed the Bluebirds from August 1910 through to May 1911 and by the 1912/1913 season he was player/manager with Newport County.

Fred STEWART

The dashing, moustachioed Mr Stewart arrived at the fledgling Bluebirds in May 1911 as their first secretary-manager, he continued up until 1933 and took the City to 2 FA Cup Finals. He once remarked that his team was full of, 'unity of feeling and purpose.' City finished third spot in his first season in charge. A part-time coal merchant whilst employed at the club, Stewart had been at Stockport for nearly twenty years previously. Upon arriving he dispensed with nearly all the playing staff. 'We get players of decent ability and each man does his best,' said Stewart in the Athletic News. He retired at the end of the '32/33 season. Mr Stewart died in 1954, he was 81.

Bartley WILSON

The 'soul and heart of the club which became Cardiff City.' Grahame Lloyd, C'mon City! author. A Bristol-born Lithographer and founder of Cardiff City Football Club, Bart took charge briefly of the playing side after Fred Stewart's departure in 1933. It was Mr Wilson that had the drive to create a football club prior to Cardiff being recognized as a city in 1905. Wilson has a gravestone at Weston cemetery in Cardiff acknowledging his founding of Cardiff City as a professional club. He died in 1954.

Jimmy Scoular

Kenny Hibbitt

Russell Osman

Richie Morgan

Ben WATTS-JONES

A founding member of Swansea Town FC prior to his arrival at City as a board member. However, he took control of the team as secretary-manager in March 1934. Jones was an FA of Wales councillor prior to this appointment and Swans chairman during the Great War. He brought in a great many new signings, amongst them Bill Jennings, a player who would eventually replace him as manager. With minimal on-field success over 3 years coupled by low attendances Mr Jones accepted a return onto the City board after his time was up in the hot seat.

Bill JENNINGS

Jennings had been a Welsh international at halfback before managing Cardiff City from 1937 through to 1939. He had risen up the ranks at Ninian Park being chief coach and the secretary-manager in 1937. He departed in April '39 and was replaced by Cyril Spiers.

Cyril SPIERS

Appointed in April 1939 any plans he had for his new team were postponed due to the outbreak of hostilities in 1939 from which point he managed the club on a part-time basis. Doing as best he could during the war years, a contract wrangle marked the Birmingham-born Spiers' departure in 1946 only for his return in 1948. His second spell in charge lasted until May 1954 with success achieved by taking City up into the First Division in the 1951/52 season. Hailed as the undisputed master builder of Cardiff City's post-world war II success, Spiers was secretary-manager at the club over fifteen-years. Cyril always wore a suit and never a tracksuit. A big, 6'1, 12 stones former keeper at Aston Villa, Spurs and Wolves, where injury curtailed his playing career and was succeeded by an assistant-managers role at Molineux. City won the Division Three South championship under him in 1947. After managing City he went on to do likewise at Crystal Palace and Exeter and at lower, non-league sides. Born in 1902 he died in May 1967.

Bill MCCANDLESS

'A man who lived for football.'
Took over the reigns at City in June 1946 due to the hasty departure of Cyril Spiers. Ulsterman Billy Mac led the team to the Third Division championship. As an Ebbw Vale player the then-40 year old 'artist', as the S.W Daily Post described him set up the winning goal in the 1926 Welsh Cup v Swansea Town. Previously having been in charge of Dundee and at nearby Newport County, the team atmosphere at Ninian Park was said to be good during his reign with competition for places proving fierce. His Newport side did the league double over City in the 1938/ 1939 season. Moving forward to Cardiff, his tenure was soon over and by late 1948 he was lured to Swansea following a lucrative cash offer. Significantly, McCandless, a manager who had no involvement with everyday training matters, collected a Third Division Championship winners medal whilst in control of Newport, Cardiff and Swansea in 1939, 1947 and 1949 respectively. Upon leaving City in November

1948 he went straight to Swansea City and managed the Swans for the next seven years. His record as City honcho reads: 100 games played, 53 won, 26 lost and 21 drawn. A City v Swansea fixture in August 1949 saw Billy presented with a gold watch as a 'thank you' from his 2 former clubs and on behalf of Newport too. He died in 1955.

Trevor MORRIS

Another of the 'guest' players for City during the War years, Morris served his time at Cardiff as assistant-secretary and then secretary-manager from 1954. Under his tutelage they were relegated to Division Two in 1957 and continued struggling there. Coming to Ninian Park in 1939, Mr Morris had been a City player until injury closed his career in 1942 and had also turned out for Ipswich Town. His departure in 1958 saw him travel up to Swansea whom he would manage over seven years as well as Newport County later. In 186 games as Cardiff City manager, Morris's team won 59, lost 87 and drew 40 matches. He won full Welsh caps as a Swansea player in the 1940s and returned their in a managerial role after leaving the Ninian Park hot spot in 1958. Awarded an OBE in 1976 Trevor Morris passed away in 2003.

Bill JONES

A great nurturer of footballing talent including a young Derek Tapscott and Alan Durban. In the mid-1950s when managing Cardiff, with previous City name Wilf Grant as his assistant, he upset many at the club by telling former fans favourites Ernie Curtis and Ron Stitfall that their services were no longer required.

Mr Jones had previously managed Barry Town and Worcester City and stayed for 4 years at City. Following his and Grant's dismissal, '27 Cup winner Ernie Curtis temporarily took control of team affairs.

George SWINDIN

A goalkeeper with Arsenal where he won club honours, his management spell at Ninian commenced in October 1962 but was not to be a happy one. With the arrival of John Charles from Italy, signed against his wishes, Swindin managed to take the club into Europe following a Welsh Cup Final success. Although he had brought in former Bluebird Stan Montgomery as trainer-coach from Norwich City [where George had been boss]. Another boss with an antiquated approach and penchant for peculiar phrases, his 18 months at the club was marked by a tough but injury-hampered squad. Of a nervy disposition, the Yorkshire man was relieved of his duties in summer 1964. Coincidentally, Mr Swindin had played for the Gunners at Ninian Park back in April 1953 in a goal-less, mid-week

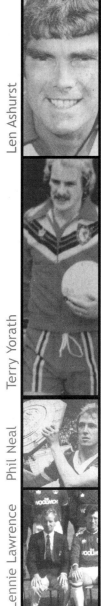

Len Ashurst

Terry Yorath

Phil Neal

Lennie Lawrence

Division One match. Swindin previously managed Peterborough.

Jimmy SCOULAR

'A much cleverer footballer than many people grant.' Billy Liddell, Liverpool & Scotland player. Scoular, nicknamed 'Iron Man' at Portsmouth as a valued player, developed a decent City side over his nine years as manager although severe training methods and a win-at-any-cost approach made him unpopular with many a City player, Ivor Allchuch in particular. The Livingstone-born Mr Scoular was a hands-on leader and would join in squad training runs. Former Bluebird defender Stan Montgomery remembers him as 'a true gent.' Under Jimmy's guidance and with full utilization of his contacts book City etched out a status as a big force in Division Two but they never made it back to Division One. 'Schoular is a hard taskmaster.' Decreed former Bluebird Ian Gibson who had been managed by the Scot at Bradford also, 'He will call at you and he will curse you on the field once off it, all is forgotten.' As City boss, he has a great Welsh Cup record, winning the trophy a lucky seven times. Scoular later moved up to the old Somerton Park to manage Newport County but quit in January 1977 following a run of poor results. A Pompey defender in his playing days back in the 1940s, Jimmy eventually retired there. In his footballing past he turned out for Scotland at Ninian Park in October 1952 v Wales where the match finished 2-2. At club level he won the FA Cup with Newcastle United in 1955. Past City skipper Sherwood returned for that same game as Wales captain. Scoular was Portsmouth boss in 1965 when City were hammered 6-1 at Ninian Park. Appointed City number one in June 1964 the year that he quit playing, Scoular left in the winter of 1973. His 9 years at the club were matched by Cyril Spiers and Fred Stewart two decades earlier. City trainer Lew Clayton took the managerial role for one match, a 2-0 defeat v Millwall before the appointment of Frank O'Farrell.

Frank O'FARRELL

'He was OK, but he was very quiet. A little too quiet.' George Best. Mr O'Farrell lasted an astounding 158 days at City after being introduced as the latest manager by then-newly installed chairman, David Goldstone. Another ex-player, he had represented the Republic of Ireland at international level and moved on to management at Leicester City. It was O'Farrell, a former Man United honcho during the declining, post-Busby years, who brought Jimmy Andrews to Ninian Park. Oddly, he was said to have a peculiar tendency for taking training whilst wearing a suit under his tracksuit. Jimmy Andrews, previously his deputy at City, was shunted into the managerial role as O'Farrell, whom it transpired, really did take the money and run. Or rather left to take up a lucrative, tax-free coaching opportunity in Iran worth a cool £20,000. City finished the season in seventeenth position, one point away from relegation.

Jimmy ANDREWS

'One of the best tactical coaches.' David Giles.

A barrel full of coaching experience coupled with a professional footballing career as a left-winger, Jimmy was tempted to leave Spurs and come to City as assistant to Frank O'Farrell. He was to be given the position of caretaker boss upon the latter's sudden departure in 1974 in a near disastrous season for the Bluebirds. Relegation called in 1975 as the club slipped into Division Three but Andrews brought the Bluebirds straight back up again. The softly-spoken Mr Andrews lost his job in October 1978 less than half-way through a supposed five year contract.

Richie MORGAN

Mr Morgan was a local lad who after signing for City in 1966 made his full debut in a 1968 European Cup Winners' Cup match with Moscow Torpedo. Prior to that game he had not even made his league debut. The solidity of a young Don Murray limited his opportunities to a total of 69 first-team appearances over a decade long career. Joining the admin staff at Ninian Park before taking up the managerial gauntlet in November 1978, Morgan succeeded in steering City to 9th in the table of Division Two for the 1978-79 season. The following season saw the squad attain a mid-table finish. Still only 34, Richie was axed after being awarded full managerial status coupled by a succession of poor results. Lesser success came for Morgan in the 1980s at Jenner Park with Barry Town.

Graham WILLIAMS

Managed the team from November 1981 through to February 1982 after being chief coach in1981. As a player, Graham was capped 26 times for Wales and won a League Cup winners medal in 1968 with West Brom and was on the losing side in the following year. An assumption is made that this was the same Williams that played for the club in the 1960s prior to a move to Bolton in October '67. As chief coach for the Bluebirds his record is brief and poor: winning one game in eleven matches. Along with the recently moved Richie Morgan, then working as general manager, both left the club in 1982. New arrival Len Ashurst took charge from March '82 onwards.

Len ASHURST

'Our task will be as difficult as anything in the past.' Ashurst, May 1982. Mr Ashurst attained stupendous success as manager of Newport County culminating with the club reaching the quarter-finals of the European Cup Winners' Cup in 1981, promotion to the Third Division and Welsh Cup winners in 1980. A former full-back, Len was replaced at Newport by future Swansea City boss Colin Addison. Moving to Ninian Park in 1982, he returned for a second spell in 1990, which saw City relegated to Division Three. [But he did bring them straight back up in the following season]. His second spell resulted in the Bluebirds sinking to Division Four. Veteran striker Bob Hatton was introduced mid-season. Ashurst left for Sunderland, where he once played, in February 1984, future City manager Frank Burrows was his assistant. He also worked at Blackpool for the 1988/ 1989 season where former City name Jimmy Mullen was boss.

Jimmy GOODFELLOW

Following Ashurst's departure, Jimmy took charge as temporary manager towards the climax of the 1983/ 1984 season working with City player Jimmy Mullen for the final two months of that campaign. Jimmy G had previously assisted Ashurst at Newport before joining the backroom staff at Ninian. Support from the board was not forthcoming during his management tenure due to his main-line inexperience. A 3-0 home defeat by Man City was the final full stop and another former Bluebirds favourite replaced him: Alan Durban. Jimmy is now back at City in the capacity of physiotherapist having been asked by Frank Burrows. As a lower leagues player he made some 500 first team appearances.

Alan DURBAN

As a fledgling Cardiff City player Mr Durban pulled on a Bluebird shirt for three years from 1959 through to 1962, making his debut in a 2-1 away win v Derby County. Nine goals in 52 games followed prior to his transfer to Derby. Coming in to take charge of City from Jimmy Goodfellow in September 1984 Durban had what can only be defined as a dog of a time as manager. Well-thought of as a young pro in his playing days at Ninian Park, Durban was sold to Derby County to raise some funds for the purchase of one John Charles. Alan arrived as new manager in September 1984 but was unable to stop City conceding to two consecutive relegations that put took the club into the Fourth Division for the first time. Hampered by serious problems at the club he was unable to make any long term plans for his team. A dire period for both the club and man, Alan Durban left in May 1986. Much-travelled player and manager, his career has taken in stints at Derby County, Shrewsbury Town, Stoke City and Sunderland. It was whilst a player-manager with Shrewsbury that Durban played against Cardiff in the 1977 Welsh Cup Final. As a Rams player he scored v City in a Division Two match at Ninian Park in '67 in a career that totalled 39 goals in two seasons at the Baseball ground.

Frank BURROWS

'You have to give him credit for putting that [the promotion winning City side of 1987/ 1988] team together with very little money.' Former Bluebird Jimmy Gilligan, Western Mail, 2004. A player and manager with a long connection to South coast clubs Portsmouth and Southampton. He played 500 games as a defender and was in the Swindon Town side that beat Arsenal in the 1969 League Cup. Burrows became City boss in May 1986 with the team in the Fourth Division and having the likes of Exeter City and Rochdale to welcome. Despite having little money to spend on new players he took the Bluebirds up in the 1987/88 season, as runners-up to Wolverhampton Wanderers as well as winning the Welsh Cup twice. His departure came in August 1989 after only two matches due to his acceptance of an assistant manager post at Portsmouth. He enjoyed four years as Swansea City boss up to 1995 and would return to Ninian Park in February 1998 and succeeded in winning promotion with the club in 1999. As a former Sunderland coach, famed for wearing a flat cap at matches, he was recommended by ex-city supremo Len Ashurst. Frank brought in the experienced Billy Ayres as an assistant, a man who knew the machinations of the lower leagues very well. Ayre also assisted Jan Molby at Swansea City. An extensive cv has seen him as coach and/or manager with clubs including Swindon Town, Portsmouth, West Ham United, Walsall. Burrows was diagnosed as having cancer of the kidney but recovered with his customary good nature retained. Took over as caretaker manager at West Brom prior to Bryan Robson's employment as new manager in November 2004 but left after rejecting a new role at the Hawthorns.

Phil NEAL

Former Liverpool defender came to City for the briefest of periods procrastinating whether or not to take over as caretaker boss of Manchester City. This he did do in October 1996. Neal was replaced by Russell Osman with City finishing 22nd in Division Three. Stepping in after the recently departed Steve Coppell, Neal didn't last long at Main Road in a year which saw the blue side of Manchester go through five separate managers. Neal assisted Graham Taylor during the latter's famed 'Do I not like that!' period as England manager.

Eddie MAY

Born in 1943, Eddie played in defence for both Wrexham (500 appearances) and Swansea prior to promotion to manager in July 1991. Formerly employed at Ninian Park as youth team coach, he played against City as a Wrexham man in the late-60s/ early-70s. He had garnered tremendous acclaim there winning promotion to Division Three in the 1969/ 1970 season, two-times Welsh Cup winner, two Wales caps and he played in the quarter-finals of the European Cup Winners' Cup. A manager at Leicester in their successful 1979/ 1980 season Eddie lasted a solitary month as Newport boss and was at Charlton Athletic with Lennie Lawrence. With the Bluebirds, May won the Third Division title in the 1992/ 1993 campaign and the Welsh Cup. He replaced Len Ashurst after being his assistant previously. May was at City from the 1991/ 1992 season onwards, [and again following his re-instatement in 1995] Recently quit as manager at Llanelli AFC, managed previously by Robbie James and Roger Gibbins.

Kenny HIBBITT

This Bradford-born Wolves playing legend spent 16 years at the Molineux club and became assistant boss to Gerry Francis at Bristol Rovers in their success period in the mid-1980s. Francis, at the tail end of his playing career, turned out a few times for City in the mid-1980s. A League Cup winner, like fellow City maestro Doug Livermore, Kenny scored against City in a league match back in the '76/ '77 season for the Wanderers, played at City's ground. In addition, he nicked another for Wolves in a 2-2 draw back in the corresponding season. As a manager of Walsall over the 1990/ 91 season Kenny returned to Ninian Park. He re-emerged to Cardiff as chief coach under a new chairman with City finishing third from bottom of Division Three in the 1995/ 1996 season. Replacing Eddie May, he was director of football in the Phil Neal debacle and was momentarily in charge prior to Russell Osman taking over. The two worked together and led the team to the play-off stages of Division Three in the 1996/ 1997 season.

Terry YORATH

Born in Cardiff, Yorath's playing career took him to Leeds, Coventry, Spurs and twice as manager of Swansea City as well as an aborted spell as City boss. Controversy and curiosity has dogged both his professional and personal life and his managerial success has proved patchy. Terry walked away from Swansea after paying up the remains of his contract personally but returned for another spell there. He came to Ninian Park after Eddie May's exit in a consortium that planned to rejuvenate Cardiff City Football Club. The bid failed and he resigned in March 1995. City were relegated from Division Two by June.

Russell OSMAN

With Kenny Hibbitt back also, this former Ipswich Town player took the Bluebirds to the play-offs before being sacked in January 1998. Russell had taken his initial shot at management at Bristol City in the early-1990s. By November '96 he had steered Cardiff to seventh in Division Three but was replaced mid-way through the season by Frank Burrows.

Alan CORK

'Corky' managed the Bluebirds from July 2001 through to February 2002 winning seventeen of his 40 games before external pressures led him to lose his job. As a player he will be remembered as an FA Cup winner with the Sam Hammam 'Crazy Gang' at Wimbledon. Prior to Ninian Park, in September 2000, Mr Cork had been in charge at the Vetch Field after the chaos of Mickey Adams's sacking had thrown the Swans into turmoil back in 1997. Adams was soon back in football, replacing Eddie May at Brentford. Alan managed the Swans for 35 games, winning 10, losing 15 and drawing the remainder. After leaving City he became assistant manager to Mickey Adams at Leicester City but both left the club in October 2004.

Lennie LAWRENCE

'I am not a quitter - I never have been.' Lawrence, a former schoolteacher, gave present City skipper Graham Kavanagh his debut at Middlesborough whilst manager there. In January 2002, his Luton Town side beat City 1-3 at Ninian Park and 2 days later Frank Burrows was sacked as City boss. Lennie was appointed as the new Director of Football for the Bluebirds in the same month. He brought his Charlton side to City for a 2-1 defeat during the 83/84 season with Eddie May his assistant.

Tarki MICALLEF

'He has fought his way into the side and is determined to stay there.' Gary Stevens, past team mate at City. Born in Cardiff in 1961, Tarki made his debut in a Cardiff shirt in 1978 and stayed with the Bluebirds until 1982. Micallef had a second and much briefer spell with City in 1984-1985 after returning from playing for Gillingham. In total, the local lad played 138 times for Cardiff City and scored 12 goals. After departing for Bristol Rovers, Tarki and eventually retired from the game in 1989 whilst with Barry Town.

Stan MONTGOMERY

'A cool stopper centre-half.'
Trevor Ford, writing in his autobiography.
'Monty' came to Cardiff as a replacement for Fred Stansfield in March 1949 and scored on his debut v Grimsby in a 2-2 draw the following January. He built up a steady stream of appearances in the number five shirt and would miss only a single match in the 1953/ 1954 season [out of a total of 42]. Overall, Montgomery notched up 243 match appearances from 1948 to 1955. His playing career was not yet over and subsequently, he made 9 appearances for Newport County before joining up with George Swindin [isn't the football world small!] at Norwich as trainer/ coach. Swindin came to manage City in 1962 and brought Montgomery with him. The ex-City stalwart went on to scout for both Bristol Rovers and City. He died in 2000.

Graham MOORE

'Tall, well-built and broad shouldered.'
A City player and full Welsh international, Moore scored a hat trick for the Bluebirds in the 1960 Welsh Cup final, the same year that saw him voted the Welsh Sports Personality of the Year. Also a former miner, Graham was capped 21 times for his country after making his debut as a teenager. It was his goal v Aston Villa which clinched promotion for the Bluebirds at the end of the 1959/ 1960 season. Celebrated by 55,000 at Ninian Park on Easter Sunday. He left to further his career with both Chelsea and Manchester United.

Graham MOSELEY

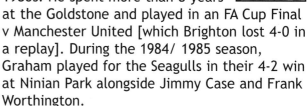

Made his debut between the sticks as a Bluebird during the 1986/ 1987 season. Cardiff became the 6th club for this Manchester-born keeper who enjoyed greatest success with Brighton & Hove Albion back in the 1980s. He spent more than 8 years at the Goldstone and played in an FA Cup Final v Manchester United [which Brighton lost 4-0 in a replay]. During the 1984/ 1985 season, Graham played for the Seagulls in their 4-2 win at Ninian Park alongside Jimmy Case and Frank Worthington.

Jimmy MULLEN

A well-travelled player and later manager, Jimmy signed for the Bluebirds in 1982 after a successful loan period from Rotherham [coincidentally, he and Ronnie Moore both played for them at that time]. He had the misfortune to join the club in the final months of a relegation-hit season in Division Two. [Although, City were the runners-up to Portsmouth in the following one]. Mullen is another well-loved City name and was the team penalty-taker whilst slotted in as a centre back for the Bluebirds over four years. He also managed Newport County after ending his playing career there after City. Jimmy spent sixteen years in the game scoring the same amount of goals, ten of them whilst at Cardiff. Along with Jimmy Goodfellow, he was briefly player-manager for the City but was not offered the role on a permanent basis. In total, he made 154 first team appearances, his first game in a City shirt being v Norwich City in March 1982. Exactly a decade later, Jimmy brought his Burnley side to play City on New Year's Day.

Don MURRAY

'One of the surest readers of the ball...' Shoot! Magazine, 1970. A super City name that made his debut aged seventeen in May 1963 v Middlesborough. Don remained at Cardiff City for over 10 seasons, playing 146 consecutive matches from 1968 - 1971. He collected 9 Welsh Cup winning medals and proved to be a major force in City's 1967 European Cup Winners' Cup surge. He was never capped by Scotland though. Murray became a centre-half stalwart for Cardiff and was considered to be more effective there than as full-back. Don proved to be a great player, making 532 appearances over 12 years. Of particular note was his ultimate performance in the Welsh Cup final against a John Charles-led Hereford United in 1968. He moved on in November 1974 for Hearts and concluded his playing life at Newport County who were managed by former City boss Jimmy Scoular.

Don had the misfortune to score an o.g in a 1-1 draw with Derby County in the 1968/ 1969 season with future City boss Alan Durban playing for the opponents.

Nicknames

The Citizens - City known as this in the programme from the 1921/ 1922 season onwards. The City - most fans refer to the club this way. Bluebirds - again springing from the illustrious team emblem.

Ninian Park GROUND

'At Ninian Park; there's no where else I'd rather be.' The original pitch sat on top of a refuse tip with ash dumped there from local factories and gasworks to create banks on either side of it. The playing surface was rough; before a match players and spectators would remove pieces of coke and glass that would come to the surface! One City player missed a piece and consequently ended up scarring his knee. A wooden stand was erected and white, wooden fencing was positioned around the pitch itself in the early days. Civic allotments were sited all around it. By the 1920s conditions at Ninian Park, originally to be titled Sloper Park, were a cause for concern. Consequently, it was decided that re-turfing was required and sea-washed turf was introduced for its apparent, associated qualities. However, years later this type of installation would be contradicted. A new dressing consisting of soil and sand was tried which gave better growth to the grass. Improvements also occurred in the Grange End of the ground and the new stand was covered. The wooden grandstand was a wooden formation which could hold 3,000 spectators as facilitated by the 1911 Wales v Scotland international played there. Both the Grange and Canton ends had turnstiles installed. Prior to the first game v Aston Villa in September 1910, some other professional / amateur games had been played at Ninian Park. It was 5 months to the day since the local council had rubber-stamped permission for Cardiff City FC to use the area as a football ground. Attendances at subsequent games were in the region of 5000. A blistering 8000 saw the 4-1 drubbing of Ton Pentre in a Southern League match. Advancing to 1924 and Ninian Park was still a primitive ground [nothing changes, does it] but 25,000 were present to watch Cardiff v Clapton [Leyton] Orient. Some 59,000 would see Chelsea beaten in the Fourth round of the FA Cup also. Apart from a small, wooden stand with a canvas roof on the Sloper road side of ground, the rest was left unprotected from the elements. Players changed in a wooden hut at the Canton End of the ground. Originally the proposed architectural plans for the new ground included a cycle track but they never materialized when work was completed in late-August 1910. A fire in January 1937 destroyed the wooden stand at the ground. Said to be the best in the country, floodlights were installed and ready for the Wednesday 24 August 1960 home match v Sheffield Wed. City lost 0-1.

1970s

'Our pitch is like a beach, any other second division player will tell you that.'

City striker Brian Clark, Goal magazine, 1972. 1972/ 1973 season - 225k spent on the main stand extension including a seating raised from 1,100 to 4,500. In 1977 - Safety of Sports Grounds Act deemed Ninian Park unsafe and consequently major reconstruction work was necessitated. Costing 600k, 200k came from the Football Grounds Improvement Trust and the FAW, which contributed 27k. City's capacity had been reduced from 46,000 to 10,000 at the time, for safety reasons. The Act saw to the demolition of the Grangetown End roof in 1977 and the reduction of its banking. The author recalls sitting on uncomfortable wooden strips for the visit of Arsenal and Southampton back in the early-1980s. Ticket admission prices to see City play were now in the region of 80p after being 6 shillings [30p] in 1970.

1980s

"I found Cardiff to be particularly intimidating,' recounts Plymouth fan Scott Chapman, 'not the most pleasant of away trips.' City fans were banned by Swansea and thus unable to attend away matches at the Vetch Field in this hooligan-strewn decade. Cardiff did likewise at Ninian Park. The 1984 Boxing Day fixture with the Swans shows the ground looking decrepit.

1990s

'...A gritty, well-sized stadium with an extremely passionate support that makes for an unforget-table experience.' Lee Roberts. August 1992 - the main stand enclosure had a new extended roof put on. The Bob Bank now had an upper section all-seated but maintaining a small standing-only section. Former Cardiff and Wales legend John Charles was the special guest of CCFC in October 1994 in a game v Crewe where he officially opened the John Charles Suite. Advancing to 1999 and the ground capacity increased to 16,500 with cash spent on the Grange End.

Ninian Park PUB

This popular watering hole used to be on the corner of Leckwith road & Wellington street. It was demolished in 1978 and now 'The Ninian' stands opposite and is a favoured spot for City fans prior to kick-off.

Kevin NUGENT

'This club is geared up for success, and there's a really great atmosphere about the place.' Commenting in October '98, Nugent completed a £65,000 move from Bristol City to Ninian Park with his debut arriving v Orient. Made club captain, he was unfortunate to miss most of the 2000/2001 season through injury. Nugent turned out as a Bluebird on 118 occasions and scored 37 goals before joining Swansea City in 1997 where he is presently a player-coach.

Russell OSMAN

'Powerful and consistent.' [Cardiff City - programme description of their future manager, then playing for Ipswich]. Remembered for his time with that club in the late-1970s, Osman played 15 times for the Bluebirds in the 1995/1996 season. He re-surfaced as a new City manager for a single month in November-December1996. Cardiff played ten times during then and won four, lost five and drew one. Osman later played for and managed, Bristol City. As an international he collected 11 caps for England.

Jason PERRY

'I learnt more playing in defence with him than at any other time in my career...' Perry on former City team mate Kevin Ratcliffe. 'Tough, uncompromising.' Radio Wales match summariser Ian Walsh. A Newport-born central defender who made his full debut for Cardiff City in as a teenager. Becoming a well-established team member by the 1989/90 season Jason proved to be a true crowd favourite. So much so that he was nicknamed 'Psycho' by the Bob Bank faithful. Jason first made his mark in a Bluebird shirt back in 1987 when he made his full debut v Exeter City. Whilst playing his club soccer with Cardiff, Perry was selected for the Wales friendly v Norway at Ninian Park in March 1994. The Red Dragons lost 1-3 but Jason acquitted himself admirably. Aged 24, it was his one and only cap, and came whilst City were playing in the old Division Two. Jason was a part of the successful double-winning side that won the Third Division Championship and Welsh Cup in 1993. With more than 300 appearances chalked up upon leaving the club, he made the short journey across the Severn Bridge to join the blue side of Bristol, namely Rovers. Now a Football Development Officer in Bridgend.

Leighton PHILLIPS

Born in Neath. Phillips made 169 appearances for the Bluebirds from making his debut v Rotherham in the 1966/1967 season. A defender-come-midfielder he was a successful player and Welsh International, with almost 500 and 58 caps respectively. Whilst at Cardiff, his first club, Leighton played in virtually every out-field position and was acknowledged as a speedy and determined athlete. He moved on up to Division One football with Aston Villa in 1974 for a fee of £80,000. Towards the end of his career in the mid-70s, he made close to a hundred appearances for Swansea City. Leighton played until 1982 and it was in his final season that he returned to Ninian Park as a Charlton player in December '81.

ASTON VILLA

LEIGHTON PHILLIPS

Keith PONTIN

Playing in the centre of the City defence his debut came in an away win at Charlton at the commencement of the 1976/ 1977 campaign. Capped twice for Wales, the 'lanky' Keith played in 40 games for the Bluebirds over the '81/ '82 relegation season. He moved on early in the next season after making 234 appearances. Pontin is one of many former Cardiff boys to see out their on field days with Merthyr Tydfil, playing over 3 seasons from 1983-1986. David Tong, Robbie James and John Charles head a list of many others formerly at Ninian Park and later Merthyr.

Kevin RATCLIFFE

'One of the toughest and quickest Cardiff

KEVIN RATCLIFFE

EVERTON

defenders for many years.' The youngest club captain to ever win the FA Cup back in 1984 at 23 years of age. Playing for Everton, Rat's men made Watford chairman Elton John cry that day by beating them 2-0. In 1985 the blue side of Merseyside won the European Cup Winners' Cup v Rapid Vienna. Athletic and professing a simple style of play that proved effective, he tried management with Chester and Shrewsbury but with little accomplishment. More recently been employed as a tv/ radio commentator for both Wales and Cardiff City games. Ratcliffe signed for the Bluebirds on a non-contract, match-by-match basis in January 1993. And in true it-can-only-happen-in-football fashion, 'Rats' headed the winner on his home debut in a 3-2 win v Carlisle United. He had previously collected his first Wales cap in an international at Ninian Park v Czechoslovakia in November 1980. That game is featured in his book Kevin Ratcliffe - My memories of Everton [see bibliography], which includes entries on his Wales appearances and others. Kevin won one cap as a Cardiff player in a match v Belgium in 1993.

Real Madrid

The quarter-finals of the European Cup Winners' Cup match with Real played in 1971 was an all-ticket game with ground tickets eventually being made available at 40p each. On their way towards the Real match, City had banished Larneca 8-0 and took care of Nantes also. The official attendance for their Spanish bout is recorded at 47,500 but realistically there were some 50,000+ present that evening. The crowd were so boisterous that the live media coverage was drowned out. Brian Clark scored an atypical centre-forward's goal with the ball coming in from the left wing and Brian climbing high in the centre of the box to nut it in. The strike came in the 12th minute and Cardiff took the tie 1-0! Real had won the first five European Cup tournaments and took the return leg at the Bernabeau by 2-0. The cup had been seen as a second-rate trophy by many at Real but in the history of Cardiff City FC that victory at Ninian Park will always be celebrated. Incidentally, looking through any club history books, the City victory is described with some derision: at one point the team are identified as English, "Real's history books are quiet on this one," writes author Phil Ball, "and mention it [the result] in passing, as if it were of no real consequence.

Gil REECE

The 'fleet-footed' Reece began his playing career at Ninian Park in the late-1950s, with two spells preceded by a time at Swansea City [he also played for Newport County]. As a 31-year-old Welsh international, he scored a hat trick for the Bluebirds in their 1973 Welsh Cup final win v Bangor. Gil had returned to City from Sheffield United and made a total of 114 appearances in a Cardiff

shirt. His full international debut came for Wales v England at City's ground in October 1965. He retired in 1976 and died in 2004.

Stan RICHARDS

'He would love to score, a great leader.'
Colin Baker, City team mate.
Holds the record for the most goals scored for Cardiff City in a single season: 30 in the championship-winning season of 1946/ 1947. Not making his debut for City until he was nearly thirty, Richards had a habit of wearing a taped-up pair of boots that had a tendency to fall apart. However, he would refuse to go out onto the pitch without them! Whenever a match went off the boil, City supporters were wont to chant to him 'Open the score'.
Stan knocked in 31 goals in 34 appearances.

Peter RODRIGUES

'Wales' Peter the Great.'
Soccer Star magazine, 1965.
As a former City defender, he was the captain of Southampton in their FA Cup winning side of 1976. Peter got his break for a Second Division City in a 3-3 away match with Sunderland in September '63. Peter played in Cardiff's opening foray of the European Cup Winners' Cup v Real Zaragoza as City took away a 2-2 draw but lost the return 1-0. It was a match attended by a near-39,000 spectators. With a Portuguese grandfather, the Spanish fans were very interested in his surname as the away game in approached.
A full Welsh international, he played against

England at Ninian in October 1965 alongside Mike England, John Toshack and Alan Durban. He was chosen on forty occasions for his country and retired from the game in 1977 after having left Cardiff for Leicester back in 1965 for a fee of £40,000.

Billy RONSON

Born near Blackpool, Ronson completed close to a hundred first team run outs at City in a period from 1979 to 1981.

Charles 'Chas' RUTTER

Who could have guessed that the gruff man selling animals in Cardiff Market was once a Cardiff City footballer? Well he was, Chas played 137 times for the Bluebirds [118 League appearances] in a 9-year career at Ninian Park. Rutter was in the City promotion winning team of the 1951/ 1952 season. That same season he gained an England 'B' cap before moving on to Exeter in 1958.

Peter SAYER

"What a thrill...it's a goal I will never forget..." Sayer quoted in the S.W Echo after scoring that goal v Tottenham. Another local lad, Sayer had a couple of spells with the Bluebirds in a career in which he enjoyed seven full Wales caps. His majestic strike against Spurs in an FA Cup match was only his second that season but it was enough to secure its inclusion in the opening titles of the BBC's Match of the Day in 1977. The game was seen by more than 27,000 at Ninian

PETER SAYER
BRIGHTON & HOVE ALBION

Park, with a famous 1-0 home victory. 'Leo' played 98 times for the club and netted twenty times over the course of his two spells with Cardiff; in 1974 and 1981. He was in the promotion-gaining City side of '75/ '76 and returned on loan, in the early-eighties. Appearing in a mere 4 games, he scored in an away match v Luton Town. Peter was transferred to Brighton & Hove Albion in 1978 for £100,000.

Alf SHERWOOD

"The finest penalty save I ever saw was by [A.S] at Anfield in 1954."

Recounts former Liverpool and Scotland legend Billy Liddell, writing in his autobiography. "Alf had gone into goal when Rolf Harris had been injury, and played as though he had spent all his life there. If Alf had not been such a splendid full back I am sure he could have held down a place with any team in goal." The save

cost Liverpool their place in Division One. A shy fellow, whose feet did all the talking signed for City in 1941 as a teen-aged amateur prior to turning pro during the war. Sherwood captained both club and country [Wales] and spent eleven years at Ninian Park spanning 1946 -1955. Born in Aberdare, he continued his Welsh connection by signing for Newport County in a career that accumulated 41 Wales caps, 6 years and more than 200 appearances for the Somerton Park side. At the time of his moving to Newport, the club were managed by former Cardiff man, Fred Stansfield. Known as the 'king of the sliding tackle' he was regarded as one of the greatest players of all time by the late Sir Matt Busby. Alf held the record as the most-capped City player with 39 international caps collected whilst playing his club football with the Bluebirds. Like many others, he had employment outside of the sport, his being working down the coalmines! A gifted all-round sportsman, Sherwood played football and cricket at international level as a boy.

He was just seventeen when he signed for the Bluebirds. A management opportunity presented itself when he took charge of Barry Town following the cessation of his kicking life.

Southern League

Prior to Cardiff being elected into the English Second Division for the 1920/ 1921 season City played in this league, alongside 21 others.

Fred STANSFIELD

'We were always good at going forward and getting stuck in although we were never dirty.' So surmised the former City captain from the late-1940s. Stansfield signed for the club in 1942 and was immediately awarded the captaincy. Fred was in the team that welcomed Moscow Dynamo to Wales for a friendly fixture in 1945. Seriously breaking his leg, his career was ruined but in spite of this, he still played for and managed Newport County in his early-thirties. He had been loaned to the club by City back in 1949.

Phil STANT

'I loved my time with Cardiff City...it was the best period of my playing career.' Signed from Mansfield Town in 1992 Phil is a former soldier who saw active service in the Falklands. City boss Eddie May brought him in as a striking partner to Carl Dale. A scorer at all his previous clubs, 'Stanty' hit the net in his debut for the Bluebirds v Hereford United in December '92. City won the match 3-2. A big success during the 1992/ 1993 season. Phil cracked in 2 hat tricks and hit a total of 19 goals that resulted in him being the top scorer at Ninian Park. Oddly, he left Ninian Park only to return once more and then be shipped out on loan. He was to play against City in a Mansfield Town side beaten 3-2 by the Bluebirds in the 1999/ 2000 season. Still in the game and playing as well, Stant was manager at Lincoln in the following season.

Eric STEELE

Kept goal for Watford at Ninian Park in the 1979/ 1980 and corresponding season. He was to come to City on loan in the 1982/ 1983 season, making seven appearances.

Gary STEVENS

'There is a touch of John Toshack about the way this lad heads the ball.' Ken Whitfield, assistant manager at Cardiff, September 1978. Initially appeared in a City shirt away to Luton Town where the team, then at the bottom of

the table, was soundly beaten 7-1. The slightly-built player scored on his home debut v Blackburn Rovers in September '78 and hit a further 50 across 160 appearances. A hat-trick v Cambridge United was recorded for the moustachioed-Stevens during the relegation season of 1981/ 1982. City won the match 5-4 with Peter Kitchen also collecting a brace. A regular on the score sheet whilst at City, Gary struck the first club goal in the 1979/ '80 season and repeated the feat in the next five consecutive matches resulting in 3 wins, a draw and one defeat. He formed the Bluebirds front line next to Tarki Micallef and Dave Bennett. Gary would leave for Shrewsbury Town by the conclusion of the'81/ '82 campaign but was back playing against City in a 2-0 defeat for the Shrews three years later.

Ron STITFALL

Born in Cardiff back in 1925, Ron played in defence and as a forward for the Bluebirds from 1947 to 1964. His brothers Albert and Robert were also on Cardiff's books during the 1950s. Stitfall was another Welsh international and City captain prior to retiring from the game in the early-1960s. Both Ron and one of his brothers played for Cardiff in a derby match v Swansea on Christmas Eve 1949. The Swans battered the Bluebirds 5-1 that day. After returning to Ninian Park a little after the end of the war in 1947, he had actually made his debut for CCFC as a lad of 14 during the war years.

Ron later coached at Newport County in the 1970s. His brace of Welsh caps came v England at Wembley (a 5-2 defeat) and against Czechoslovakia at Ninian Park, which Wales won 1-0 in May '57. In all, Ron made more than 400 appearances for the Bluebirds. By the early-1970s he was at Somerton Park as a trainer with Newport.

Lord Ninian Edward CRICHTON STUART

'Colonel Kindness.' The 2nd son of the 3rd Marquess of Bute, owner of Cardiff Castle, officially opened Ninian Park on 1 September, 1910. The club was required to advocate a sponsor that would underwrite the £90 p.a rent charged by the council for the waste ground. As guarantor, the powers within the club offered to name the ground after him and hence Ninian Park was chosen. Crichton-Stuart officially began City's life there with the 5pm kick off on that Autumnal day in 1910 friendly fixture against Aston Villa. Born in 1883, his family name dates back to 1488, with the family being prominent in Cardiff back in the c.18th. A keen sportsman, Lord Ninian spent much of his childhood in Cardiff and became its elected Conservative MP in 1910. The moustachioed, debonair Lord was killed in the Battle of Loos, Belgium, during the Great War of 1914-1918. Coincidentally, Bart Wilson's son also lost his life in the conflict and in total, 6 MPs were killed in the conflict. A statue of Crichton Stuart can be found in the gardens directly in front of the National Museum.

Derek SULLIVAN

'An immediate success, his cultured left-foot

adding an extra dimension to a stereotyped team overcrowded with right-footers.' Another Wales International whilst at City, the Newport-born Sullivan played in nearly all out-field positions for the Bluebirds. Making his debut v Newcastle United in April 1948 when Cardiff finished the season 5th in Division Two. He finally gained some consistency over the 1952/ '53 campaign even netting the winner v Burnley watched by 33,413 in the following season home fixture. Sullivan was in the Wales side that played in the 1958 World Cup finals in Sweden. He originally joined the Bluebirds as a junior, collecting 2 Welsh Cup Winners medals and a promotion medal coupled by a total of 285 appearances. After playing in all but the centre forward and goalkeeper positions he left the club during the 1960/ 1961 season after playing his final game in a City shirt in an 3-2 away defeat at Spurs. Derek died in 1983.

Mel SUTTON

As a midfielder, Mel [pictured opposite] turned out for Cardiff, Wrexham and Aston Villa. Playing for the Bluebirds for the first time in August 1968 he soon became a familiar name on the team sheet over the coming four seasons. He played for Cardiff 178 times and left the club for another Welsh side; Wrexham.

Swansea TOWN / Swansea CITY

A founder member of Division 3 the club were originally called Swansea Town.

Ex-Bluebird and Wales manager, John Toshack joined them in 1978 and their incredible climb up to finishing sixth in Division One soon followed. At the end of the 1977/ 78 season they won promotion to Division Four. In the next they went up to Division Three, won the Welsh Cup and promotion to Division Two in the 1980/ 81 season, and finished 6th in Division One in the next season. In the 1983/ 84 Swansea won the Welsh Cup. Trevor Ford, John & Mel Charles and Ivor Allchurch were all Swansea players prior to moving to City, except John Charles. City bosses Alan Cork and Frank Burrows all had spells in the Swans hot seat.

City v Swansea matches

The first match between Cardiff and Swansea Town, as they then were, occurred in a Southern League Division Two fixture on 7 September 1912. Staged at the Vetch Field, the game finished all equal at 1-1. The first played at Ninian Park was a Welsh Cup semi-final clash in February 1913 which Swansea won 2-4. The clubs have met on many occasions over the years, and from 1912 to 2002 there were 150 matches and so, here are just a few gems. 27/08/1949 - In the season that saw Swansea win the Welsh Cup managed by future Bluebirds manager Billy McCandless, Cardiff took the honours 1-0 in front of 57,510.

24/12/1949 - Ivor Allchurch makes his full debut for the Swans in a commendable 5-1 trouncing at the Vetch. A 16-year-old amateur called John Charles heads off to Leeds United from the competition winners.

23/02/1950 - The Welsh Cup quarter-finals sees City lose 1-0 to Swansea Town in front of a crowd numbering 65,855. The following match found Swans boss Billy McCandless presented with a gold watch to commemorate his achievement in winning three separate championships whilst with Cardiff, Newport and Swansea respectively.

30/04/1956 - The Welsh Cup Final. Kicking off at 6.30 pm at Ninian Park, 37,500 were present in advance of a 3-2 home win for the Bluebirds. City destroyed Oswestry Town 7-0 whilst the Swans took care of Newport County 5-2 in the corresponding semi-finals.

1957/ 1958 season - City v Swansea draw watched by 40,000.

7/03/1959 - Division Two match played at Ninian Park records the first ever league goal and victory attained by Swansea Town against the Bluebirds in this match.

2/02/1960 - City field a team of reserves in a wet and muddy Welsh Cup 6th round defeat of Swansea at the Vetch Field. In what was a hilarious affair for all the wrong reasons, City's Mokone and the Swans own Griffiths were dismissed for throwing mud at one another. This was after they had already completed a physical grapple!

6/04/1965 - Cardiff City 5 v Swansea 0. A smashing result for the Bluebirds in a Division Two match that allowed City to stay up and sank Swansea to Division Three. Ivor Allchurch grabbed a hat trick and John Charles produced a wonderful 'net buster'.

1/01/1980 - The first league encounter between the clubs in 15 years sees a 1-1 ending. David Giles strikes for Swansea, his first since returning from Wrexham. John Toshack plays against his hometown club as the Swans player-manager. [pictured below opposite]

20/09/1988 - Swansea City 0 v Cardiff City 2. The City record their first win at the Vetch Field in 30 odd years in a League Cup 1st round, 2nd leg tie.

7/03/1995 - Division Four fixture between a lowly-placed Cardiff and promotion-seeking Swansea concludes in a 4-1 home win for the latter. An orange ball is used due to the pitch being carpeted in snow and hail.

12/ 12/ 1996 - Swansea beat Cardiff 3-1 at Ninian Park. 'They [Cardiff City] were 5 points ahead of us with a game in hand...' recounts Jan Molby, the former Liverpool star became the Swans player-manager in February 1996. 'We came of age against Cardiff. We won quite comprehensively with a very impressive performance...'

2/03/1999 - Cardiff City 3 v Swansea City 2.

In the FAW Premier Cup quarter-finals, ex-Swan Dai Thomas scores for City. After being shown the door by the Bluebirds Thomas made the headlines for his involvement in off the pitch activities some time later. He was convicted as a football hooligan.

13/05/2002 - Cardiff City 1 v Swansea City 0. The Welsh Cup is then re-titled the FAW Premier Cup and is won by a single goal from City captain Graham Kavanagh. Cardiff had seen off Wrexham in the semi-final and the Swans had beaten Barry Town in their corresponding tie.

Derek TAPSCOTT

'It was as good as playing football. It's been great doing it.' A humble Derek Tapscott after signing copies of his autobiography at the Cardiff City shop in November 2004. Known as 'Tappy', when in front of goal this Barry-born striker was said to be equally brilliant or dreadful, depending upon what he did with the ball. A physical competitor in the days when football really lived up to the description, Tapscott enjoyed seven years with City after signing from Arsenal. As is the irony often found in the sport, it was against his former club that he scored the controversial winner against in a 1-0 victory at Ninian Park. The Gunners were furious after believing that he had handled the ball on its way into the goal; Derek said nothing and it was allowed to stand. A real smiley-smiley character and scorer of many a goal in the days when the body checking of opposing goalies was accepted in the British game, Tappy moved on to Newport County in 1965 after notching up seventy nine goals in 194 appearances. He was equally at home as either an inside-right or centre-forward. Derek played as an Arsenal man in the losing Welsh team v Scotland in 1954. Madly enough, Tappy played 5 games for City with a broken foot in the 1963/ 64 season!

Rod THOMAS

Amassed club success at Swindon Town and Derby County before coming to Wales and signing for Cardiff in October 1977. Rod was a decent utility player and could fit in equally well in any defensive position. A Welsh international to boot, Thomas played 96 times for the Bluebirds over 4 years.

David TONG

'Football is a crazy game.' Tong commenced his playing career with Cardiff City in 1982 with his debut arriving in a 2-1 defeat by Wrexham on the first day of that promotion-attaining season. David notched up 141 games in a Blue shirt. He played for Shrewsbury Town against City during the 1981/ 1982 season. By the mid-1980s he was in the same Merthyr Tydfil team as another ex-Bluebird, Keith Pontin.

John TOSHACK

'Tosh was a one-off.' Kevin Keegan. Toshack used to watch City play from the Grange End as a lad before signing as an apprentice for the club in June 1965. His full debut came v Middlesborough, in a 4-3

JOHN TOSHACK

away match where he scored twice. In 1966, as a youngster fresh from the reserves the now professional John initially found the change of pace difficult to acclimatize to. His signing for City would never have happened if Leeds United had had their way after he was spotted by the same scout that recommended John Charles to the Elland Road club. However, John chose to follow his heart and signed on for his hometown team.

By twenty-one he accepted a transfer to Liverpool for £110,000 after previously declining a similar move to Fulham. The bulk force of Alan Warboys was brought in to replace him in the City front line and Alan netted all 4 goals in the defeat of Carlisle at Ninian Park. During his Liverpool playing days, John was so popular that he even had his own Christmas annual; whilst most of us looked forward to a Shoot! one, the "Tosh" offering came out in 1978. A book of his poetry, Gosh it's Tosh was also published. A fabulous City name John was born in 1948 he would move on to make an international name in a formidable goal-scoring partnership with Kevin Keegan at Liverpool. But that came later and back at Ninian Park, just over nine thousand saw him as a sixteen-year-old make his full home debut against Leyton Orient in

November '65, scoring one of the goals in a 3-1 win. Cardiff finished 20th in Division Two that season with the teen-aged 'Tosh' netting six times. Said to be sold because Cardiff did not want to be seen as a lesser force than one of its players, or could it just have been that 110k was just too good to turn down? Whatever, in true style he bowed out by scoring a hat trick in his last game at Ninian Park for the Bluebirds v Hull City in October 1970. Writing in his autobiography, Toshack retells the Boxing Day 1983 tale when Cardiff were pitted against Swansea at Ninian Park. Football being as football is, Tosh picked himself after an absence of nearly three years and what happens? He get's the ball from the halfway line and moments later it ends up in the top corner of the City net! The former Bob Bank idol received a torrent of abuse from the home fans as a result. He both played for and managed, Swansea City during their formidable rise and fall years of the late-70s/ early-80s. Toshack's playing career statistics are impressive: 204 apps/100 goals for Cardiff City, 245 appearances/ 95 goals for Liverpool, 69 appearances / 30 goals for Swansea City and 40 appearances / 10 goals for Wales. Still coaching, he intermittently appears as a sour-faced tv pundit covering Welsh internationals. In November 2004, Tosh was appointed the new manager of the Wales national side. He had managed the side some years earlier but resigned after one game [v Norway].

'One, two, three...it's Tosh!' A City programme headline re: Toshack hat trick v Q.P.R in

September 1969, the season that saw him top scorer in the whole division with 22 goals.

Billy THIRLAWAY

Bill was in the City team that won the FA Charity Shield in the 1927/ 1928 season. He scored 9 goals in Division One after joining the club in March 1927.

Regrettably ineligible for the FA Cup Final with Arsenal due to playing in the earlier rounds whilst with Birmingham City.

Nigel VAUGHAN

'I'm never happy with anything less than my best.' Vaughan quoted in 1980 as an established Newport County player.

Quite a goal-scorer in his time with 42 netted as a City player over the seasons 1983 to 1987. His Bluebirds debut came in a dire 3-0 defeat by Burnley and he led the goal scoring chart for the club in his first 2 seasons at Ninian Park both of which, resulted in relegation! Nigel had made his name as a midfielder for over eight years with the Len Ashurst-led Newport County where he had been signed as a schoolboy.

A diminutive and responsive City player, who appreciated the attention of City fans, Nigel played over 149 times for Cardiff and was a full Welsh international.

He achieved success with Wolves after leaving the Welsh club, with whom he won 2 league championships. Ironically, his debut for the Wanderers came against Cardiff City at Ninian Park, where he came on as a late substitute and saw his side win 3-2. He netted ten times in 93 appearances for the Wolves.

Opposite: Brian Walsh

Graham VEARNCOMBE

Here's a player with a unique story to be told; Vearncombe was a Cardiff-born lad that made his full City debut in 1953.

However, as a consequence of a pay dispute, he left the club and went to sea for six months only to return and finally play again for the Bluebirds in 1959! Graham collected 2 full Welsh international caps and left Ninian Park in 1964 after keeping goal for City on more than 200 occasions. As with innumerable other past Cardiff City names, Vearncombe played for Merthyr Tydfil as his career wound down in the 1970s.

Harry WAKE

It was Wake's error that allowed the Sheffield United player Fred Turnstall to score v City in the 1925 FA Cup Final. He had made his debut for the Bluebirds a year before and was unlucky enough to be injured when the club returned to Wembley for the victorious 1927 final win v Arsenal. Despite all the bad luck, Harry struck many important goals for City.

Brian WALSH

A great out and out striker and thinking past his sell-by date, Brian qualified as an accountant during his time with City! He was a part of the Cardiff side that won the Welsh Cup in the 1955/ 1956 campaign, scoring twice in the 3-2 win v Swansea Town. Arriving from Arsenal his debut came v Preston North End and he played in a City team that experienced mediocre times on the field [relegation and mid-table positioning] until promotion was gained from Division Two in the 1959/ '60 season. Great on the ball, his prowess was appreciated by the Ninian faithful over the course of a half dozens years spent as a Bluebird. Consistent in holding on to the number seven shirt, he remained at the club until October 1961 wherein he left for Newport County and retired thereafter. This was not before contributing to the City team that once again won the Welsh Cup in 1958/ 1959. In total, Brian played 240 times for City and scored 41 goals. He died in 2001.

Alan WARBOYS

'Everything I hit went in.' Warboys commenting about his 4 goals scored v Carlisle United in the 1970/ 1971 season seen by 22,502 at Ninian Park.

A strong striker who scored on his Ninian Park debut against his former club, Sheffield Weds, in December 1970 (he'd only arrived that month) Alan was not with the Bluebirds so very long, leaving after 73 appearances had netted him 28 goals. Highlights of his time with City include his 13 strikes [in 17 matches] during the 1970/ 1971 season. Another hat trick was collected v Preston North End in that same season. Over a long career, he completed 482 games, scoring 137 goals at a total of 7 clubs. Warboys played for Bristol Rovers in a 0-2 win at City in 1976. He then

returned to Ninian Park some days later for a league match, which Rovers won 1-2. He also scored in the same match!

Johnny WATKINS

A natural left-footer, Watkins played alongside Brian Walsh in the Cardiff front line of the mid-1950s. As an integral part of the side, he saw success with the Bluebirds as they gained promotion to Division One in the 1959/60 season. Cardiff were runners-up to Aston Villa [with one point separating the two] and Johnny was an ever-present figure all season bar the final game. His City career was sandwiched between periods with both the Bristol clubs. He wore the Blue shirt 69 times and netted seventeen goals.

The Welsh CUP

The Welsh Football Association Challenge Cup came in to creation in 1877. Not the oldest cup competition, the FA Cup holds that honour, the first Welsh Cup was won by Wrexham. A handsome-looking object, the cup measured 2ft 6inches and was originally made by Bensons of London's Old Bond street. Initial seasons of the competition saw clubs being organized in to geographical gatherings. Cardiff first won the trophy in the 1912/13 season. That season was also noteworthy in that Swansea Town AFC was formed. The Swans met Cardiff in the semis seen by 12,000 at Ninian Park. City were then top of the Division Two Southern League whilst their opponents were 8th. Swansea won 2-4 and went on to win the cup. By 1995, winning the Welsh Cup no longer meant an automatic place in the European Cup Winners' Cup.

1919/ 1920 - Cardiff v Swansea: the sides had met on four occasions already that season, winning twice each prior to meeting in the semi-finals. City won the cup.

1955/ 56 - Cardiff beat Swansea by a 3-2 scoreline seen by 37,600. Mel Charles is in the losing side that evening where a programme cost threepence. Brian Walsh hits two.

1960 - Cardiff City FC was fined 350 guineas by the FAW for not fielding their first team in a Welsh Cup match v Swansea. The Bluebirds still ran out winners in a nasty, physical match. City's validation for sending the first team players is explained due to City having a league match with Leyton Orient two days after the Cup tie. And as they were pushing for promotion to Division One this was understandable. It made no difference as Cardiff lost the final anyhow.

From 1961, winning the Welsh Cup meant entry into the European Cup Winners' Cup but by the mid-1990s its interest had waned with a European place no longer a right.

1963/ 64 season - City face a Bangor team in the final managed by Tommy Jones, who was going to be the next Cardiff manager in late 1962 but failing to agree terms, George Swindin landed the job instead. City won the match and were automatically in the forthcoming European Cup Winners' Cup tournament.

1964/ 65 season - Cardiff make it to the final again. Ivor Allchurch is the shining star for the City side against Wrexham.

1966/ 67 season - City defeat Hereford United in the final 6-1 on aggregate whilst on the way to an ugly final v Wrexham.

1967/ 68 season - City v Hereford in the final. Cardiff come away with the trophy. Previous Ninian Park favourite John Charles, is a player-manager for Hereford that season. The magic still glistens and he even makes it on the score sheet. Even if Charles' team then playing in the Southern League, had won the cup, they would not have been eligible to compete in Europe as they were a non-Welsh side.

1968/ 69 season - Cardiff v Swansea in the final. John Toshack, then more than a decade away from returning to the Vetch as boss hits his 30th goal of the season in a Bluebirds shirt. City turn out winners.

1969/ 70 season - Brian Clark nest 5 times on the way to the final which City win over two-legs v Chester. Back in European football once again, the Bluebirds win the Welsh Cup trophy for the fifth time.

1970/ 71 season - City's sixth final appearance in seven years sees them defeat Wrexham. Future Cardiff manager Eddie May plays for the opposition.

1971/ 72 season - Wrexham beat City in the final. The North Wales side notch up their eighteenth Welsh Cup final win, to City's sixteen. Still in the Wrexham side, Eddie May collects a winners medal. Both teams had narrowly avoided relegation in the league. The win marks the first European entry for Wrexham.

1972/ 73 season - City play their 1964 final opponents Bangor in the final. The Bluebirds are victorious thanks to a three-goal strike by Gil Reece.

1973/ 74 season - Early round tie v Ton Pentre is recorded as the lowest-ever City match attendance. Cardiff win the cup once again.

1974/ 75 season - Wrexham beat City over a two-leg final.

1975/ 76 season - City storm back and win the trophy v Hereford after an April 2-2 draw at Ninian Park is deemed void. The FAW having discovered that Hereford had fielded an ineligible player.

1976/ 77 season - A Cardiff v Shrewsbury Town final. Ex-Bluebird and future managerial disaster Alan Durban appears for the Shrews and wins a medal as City are defeated.

1980/ 81 season - City v Swansea City final. It's Cardiff City's first appearance since 1977, as a crowd of 15,000 are present at the Vetch Field to see a Swansea victory. The Swans retained the trophy in the following season.

1987/ 88 season - Cardiff face Wrexham in the final. City had not beaten their opponents in the 2 previous league games that season. The Bluebirds come out winners with former Swansea favourite Alan Curtis netting once.

1990/ 91 season - Swansea City win the Cup under Frank Burrows.

1991/ 92 season - City face Barry Town at the National Stadium in the final. Former City player Neil O'Hallaran is then chairman of Town with Terry Boyle and Alan Curtis in amongst their victorious squad that afternoon.

1992/ 93 season - Cardiff win the 106th final in a 5-0 win v Rhyl at the National Stadium.

2001/ 02 season - Cardiff win the FAW Premier Cup with a 1-0 victory brought by a Graham Kavanagh goal.

Leo FORTUNE-WEST

'Very strong and holds the ball up well and is a constant menace to defences...'
Big Leo signed for Cardiff City from Rotherham United in September 2000. It was his seventh club in a career that has since taken its latest step when he moved on to Doncaster Rovers for the 2004/ 2005 season. LFW was introduced as a Cardiff City player v Halifax Town in a game that he managed to grab a goal in the Bluebirds' 4-2 win. He walked off with a hat trick v Hull City in a 2001 fixture. Never regarded as anything other than an old fashioned striker, Leo made many appearances as a substitute before moving on from the club.

Gareth WILLIAMS

London-born Gareth took on the City captaincy in 1964, some 3 years after his arrival at the club. The midfield dynamo, was eventually transferred to Bolton Wanderers for £45,000. He made his debut for the Bluebirds v Bournemouth and scored 14 goals in 161 first-team appearances collected over 3 seasons. Now runs a bar in Gran Canaria.

Roley WILLIAMS

Born in Swansea, Williams made his playing debut in a Bluebird shirt in 1949 and notched up 143 appearances and 19 goals. He was also a part of the 1951/ 52 promotion-winning side. After leaving Ninian in 1956 he played against City for Lowell's in the '59 Welsh Cup Final.

Bob WILSON

'A lanky young goalkeeper.' Keeper that played a big role in some prosperous periods enjoyed by Cardiff City FC. He won 2 Welsh Cup Winners medals and played for the club in their early forays in the European Cup Winners' Cup. It was his mistake that resulted in a 2-3 defeat by Hamburg SV in that said cup.

George WOOD

Now the goalkeeping coach at Ninian Park Wood maintained a high pedigree of success as player for all the clubs he served. Brought to Cardiff whilst Frank Burrows was manager, George arrived in January 1988 as cover for the recently retired Graham Moseley and subsequently played his part in the Welsh Cup and Division Four promotion-winning squad of the early-1990s. In all, he kept goal for City on

92 occasions in a career that encompassed Blackpool, Arsenal, Everton and Crystal Palace. He played against the Bluebirds on a number of occasions at Ninian Park, whilst number 1 at Crystal Palace, Blackpool and Hereford.

Bobby WOODRUFF

'A skilful midfield operator with pace and vision.' Also a very

fine goal scorer in City colours and for all the other clubs that he turned out for i.e. Swindon, Wolves and Crystal Palace. Bobby came to Ninian Park in the late-1960s for a fee of £25,000. Concluding 5 years at the club he moved on to Newport County in the summer of 1974 after hitting 22 goals across 150 appearances. Similarly adept with a long throw ala Andy Legg, one measured 41 yards. He was still playing in 1983 when he turned out for Newport in the Welsh Cup.

Billy WOOF

Came to Cardiff on a trial basis under manager Len Ashurst in September '82. On loan from Middlesborough player, he scored for the City in their 3-2 win over Wigan after an injury to Jeff Hemmerman resulted in Woof's earlier than anticipated baptism into the first team. With Hemmerman being fit for the next match, Woof was furious that he had lost his place and a fall out with the boss resulted in him leaving after a single match in City colours!

Terry YORATH

"The skipper to Wales that Bobby Moore had been to England." Michael Boon, writing in the Western Mail. 'A natural leader, and one of the main characteristics you need for that is honesty.' Brian Flynn, Wales team mate. Born in Cardiff,

Yorath's career took him to Leeds, Coventry, Spurs and twice as manager of Swansea as well as an aborted spell as City boss. Presented with the captaincy of the national team on some 42 occasions, Terry collected 59 caps in all. His time as Wales manager culminated in that Paul Bodin penalty miss. Now assistant manager with Huddersfield Town, in his playing days Terry proved to be a versatile, determined and physical competitor who put in appearances in all 10 outfield positions during his days at Leeds' Elland road. Yorath played for his country under the management of former City and Spurs player Mike England. His brother, David, was also on the books at Cardiff City. Terry's autobiography Hard Man, Hard Knocks was published in 2004.

Scott YOUNG

Another in a long and celebrated line of Cardiff greats. Scott signed as a schoolboy with City in January 1990 and made his first team debut v Stockport in 1993. Young played under 10 different mangers whilst at Ninian Park for more than a decade. It will be for that winning goal in the thrilling 2002 FA Cup victory v Leeds United that he will forever be remembered. He was awarded a testimonial by the club in August 2003.

Football League Division II.   Saturday, 7th March 1959.
Kick-off 3.15 p.m.
CARDIFF CITY v **SWANSEA TOWN**
Board of Directors : Sir HERBERT MERRETT, J.P. (President); R. BEECHER (Chairman)
F. T. DEWEY, J.P., G. EDWARDS, M.A.   Secretary : C. E. SARGENT.
Manager : W. JONES
Registered Office : NINIAN PARK · CARDIFF.

The Cardiff City and Swansea town team line-ups for the Welsh Cup Final at Ninian Park, 8 February, 1966.

BIBLIOGRAPHY AND REFERENCES

For Club & Country - Welsh Football Greats. Ed. Peter Stead, Univ of Wales Press, 2000.
The History of the Welsh Cup 1877 - 1993, Ian Garland, Bridge Books, 1993.
Born Under a Grange End Star, David Collins, Sigma Leisure 2002.
Guinness Football Encyclopeadia, Guinness.
The South Wales Derbies: A History of Cardiff City v Swansea City. Dean P Hayes, Parrswood, 2003.
Passovotchka: Moscow Dynamo in Britain 1945. David Downing, Bloomsbury, 1999.
One Cap Wonders - The Ultimate Claim to Football Fame, Grahame Lloyd, Robson Books, 2001.
When Pele Broke Our Hearts - Wales & the 1958 World Cup, Mario Risoli, Ashley Drake Publishing, 1998.
Football Stars of the 70s & Where Are They Now? Dean P Hayes, Sutton Pub., 2003.
Swansea City 1912 - 1982 - David Farmer, Foreword by John Toshack, Pelham, 1982.
Welsh Sporting Greats, ed by Alun Wyn Bevan, Gomer, 2001.
Tosh, John Toshack autobiography.
The Tosh Annual, Duckworth, 1978.
Cardiff City F.C: An A to Z, Dean Hayes, Aureus, 1998.
The Archive Photographs - CCFC 1947-1971. Compiled by Richard Shepherd, Chalford, 1997.
CCFC 1971 -1993, ditto.

BIBLIOGRAPHY

Kevin Ratcliffe - My Memories of Everton, Britespot, 2004.
I Lead the Attack, Trevor Ford, Stanley Paul, 1957.
CCFC: The Official History of the Bluebirds. John Crooks, Yore, 1992.
A Who's Who of Cardiff City Footballers, ditto.
Derby County - The Clough Years, Michael Cockayne, Parrs Wood Press, 2003.
White Storm : 100 Years of Real Madrid, Phill Ball, 2002, Mainstream Publishing
C'mon City! A Hundred years of the Bluebirds, Grahame Lloyd, Seren, 1999.
Jan the Man: From Anfield to the Vetch Field, Jan Molby with Grahame Lloyd, Orion 1999.
History of Newport County F.C - 1912 - 1973, Richard Shepherd, Newport Reference Library.
The King:Denis Law- autobiography, Bantram 2003.
Who's Who of Welsh International Soccer Players, Gareth M Davies & Ian Garland, Bridge Books, 1991
Football League Players Records 1946 - 1992, ed.Barry J. Hugman,
Tony Williams Publications,   1992.
Billy Liddell, My Soccer Story, S Paul, 1960.
John Charles-Gentle Giant, Marlo Risoli, M/stream.
Bestie - A Portrait of a Legend.
The Authorized biography of George Best, Joe Lovejoy, S&J, 1998.
Red Dragons in Europe: A Complete Record, Terry Grandin, Desert Island Books, 1999.

A Game of Two Halves, Mandarin, 1992, ed. Stephen F. Kelly. Ivan Sharpe article.
The Robin Friday Story - The Greatest Footballer You Never Saw, Paul McGuigan & Paolo Hewitt, Mainstream Publishing.
England! England! Complete Who's Who of players since 1946, Dean P.Hayes, Sutton Publishing, 2004.
Tappy: From Barry Town to Arsenal, Cardiff City and Beyond, Derek Tapscott, 2004.The Wolves Who's Who, Tony Matthews, Britespot, 2001.

Thanks to Dave in Cardiff, for access to the pictures and his excellent website. Check out his Cardiff Cards site @ http://uk.geocities.com/cardiffcitycards/ for a plethora of City items.
Also, thank you to Phil + everyone that helped with regards to loaning programmes and expressing their enthusiasm about City.

WEDNESDAY, 11th MARCH, 1970
VERSUS
SWANSEA CITY
KICK-OFF 7.30 p.m.

BLUEBIRDS
1/-
JOURNAL

CARDIFF CITY FOOTBALL CLUB

Division 2

v. Swansea City